MASKS, MUMMIES, AND MAGICIANS

A Voyage of Exploration in
Pre-Inca Peru

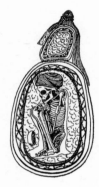

MASKS, MUMMIES, AND MAGICIANS

A Voyage of Exploration in
Pre-Inca Peru

SIMONE AND ROGER WAISBARD

Translated by
PATRICIA RUSSELL

OLIVER & BOYD

EDINBURGH AND LONDON

1965

OLIVER AND BOYD LTD

Tweeddale Court
Edinburgh, 1

39A Welbeck Street
London, W 1

Translated from the French
La vie splendide des momies péruviennes
René Julliard, Paris

First English Edition, 1965

Printed in Great Britain
by T. and A. Constable Ltd, Hopetoun Street
Printers to the University of Edinburgh

PREFACE

These lines are intended to express both my own and my colleagues' gratitude for the great interest in our work shown by Simone and Roger Waisbard. They also bear witness to the enthusiasm with which the authors set about their task of achieving the most thorough possible documentation of this work. They were present while we were digging and restoring, and have had access to all our notes and records.

They have worked tirelessly to gather evidence to illustrate and support their own personal theories.

As a Peruvian I am impressed by their love of my country and I am convinced that their book will arouse in many hearts an echo of the enthusiasm which they themselves have shown for the ancient days of Peru.

ARTURO JIMENEZ-BORJA

CONTENTS

ILLUSTRATIONS

HALF-TONE PLATES

Text Figures

Maps

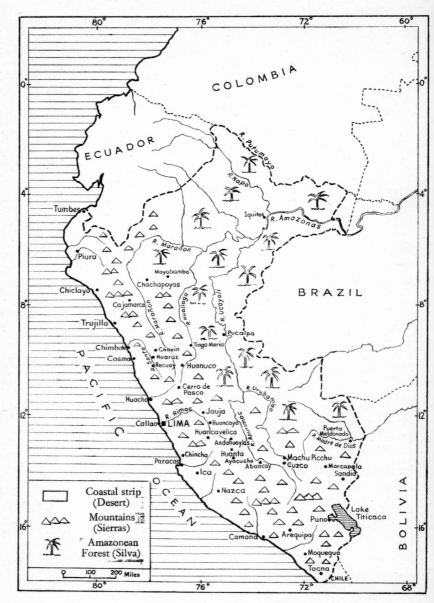

PERU: LAND OF MUMMIES

I

PERU: LAND OF MUMMIES

'There is really remarkably little known about the very early days of Lima . . .', writes Quesada at the beginning of his recent book on Lima and its surrounding oasis, that green valley dotted with pyramids arising from the desert sands. So little indeed that this great Peruvian historian was content to sum up in five pages all that is known of the pre-Inca period of his ancient city.

Many centuries before the famous Incas ruled over their mighty domain, however, the Lima valley, facing on to the Pacific Ocean, was peopled by ancient tribes whose history has remained until our own day buried under the white sands of the coast. So that when more than four hundred years ago Pizarro and his Spanish *conquistadores* ventured there, the Indians whom they found in the country had little recollection of the successive waves of archaic tribes who had preceded them; and now even the history of these same Indians —so much nearer to our own day—together with most of the details of the Spanish conquest, have come down to us in a few sparse documents written in an ancient form of Spanish which is very hard to interpret accurately.

This, therefore, is the story of a part of history—or earlier prehistory—which has never before been written. We shall do our best to follow its trail through the picture-puzzle chronicles of the sixteenth century, and in and out of the mysterious secular rites which have come to our knowledge. It is the fascinating exploration of a bygone age where those whom we seek are no longer the Indians we know today, resplendently plumed in their multicoloured *ponchos*, but characters whose silence will never be broken: the mummified figures of their ancestors.

There are literally thousands of these mummies, crouching throughout the centuries beside all the objects which in life symbolised their religion, their pleasure, their work, or their wealth: here is an empty gourd which still holds some grains of maize; bowls from which the divine ritual drink of *chicha* has long since evaporated; finely woven work-baskets where we may still find bobbins of coloured cotton, sewing and embroidery needles, spindles and looms, and brightly coloured squares of material. Here also are bamboo cases of red or blue make-up; little tweezers made of gold or silver; combs fashioned from sturdy thorns; tapestry satchels containing *coca* leaves (used as a stimulant), and the tiny scales for weighing out the quantities required; flutes of bone whose three notes must have rung out and enchanted the landscape of a civilisation long since dead. Here and there are caskets of painted and carved wood, containing necklaces of tiny beads carved from sacred shells, or mysterious idols moulded in clay. All these were the spiritual necessities, the symbolic nourishment required for the Other World by a world already extremely old—the world into which we are going to launch ourselves on a voyage of exploration.

*   *   *

To the best of our knowledge not one of the pharaohs of Egypt or their descendants ever had the fantastic idea of building his house on top of the Great Pyramid. Had this sacrilege been attempted it would surely have been vehemently attacked, and the mortal vengeance of some infuriated Tutankhamen vowed upon its progenitor. Nevertheless, many thousands of miles away from ancient Egypt this idea did occur to one of the descendants of the no less famous Incas—for Peru is still, to most people, the land of the Incas. It is not generally known that even before the Inca dynasty of Tahuantinsuyo there was another highly cultured race living in the narrow valleys of the desert shore which runs along the Pacific coast in the shadow of the Andes. Indeed it is only recently that historians, archaeologists, and other scholars interested in the history of this part of America have revealed to the world the heights of artistic perfection attained by the pottery, woven cloth, and metal-work of these people—the Mochicas and Chimus from the north, and the Nazca-Paracas of the south, who were living in Peru between two and three thousand years ago.

It was probably towards the end of the eleventh century A.D. that the powerful Tiahuanaco empire, which occupied the high plains of our present Bolivia, had its greatest cultural influence on the peoples of the coast. Their loss of power three centuries later was followed by a renaissance of the original arts of the coastal region. This was modified in the second half of the fifteenth century by the invasion of the Incas, whose civilisation was itself to be interrupted a hundred years later by the Spanish conquest.

So much is clear from a study of the races who occupy the northern and southern regions today. But until quite recently nothing was known at all of the people of the central region, the area around what is now Lima, whose cities and pyramids were as splendid as those of the north, whose tombs and mummies as fascinating as those of the south, and who had acquired considerable skill in painting in dazzling colours on fine silks and cottons.

We must therefore render due praise to the imaginative citizen of Lima who, by planning a modern villa on the site of one of the ancient sacred pyramids, unwittingly revealed to us a clue to the finding of his prehistoric ancestors, hidden until that day beneath the ever-moving wind-blown sands of the Pacific coast. True, it was an extraordinary looking pyramid, so misshapen that a passer-by might well have taken it for one of the 'artificial hills' mentioned by the chroniclers of Pizarro, so lost in oblivion that no one even knew the primitive name of this mound, which rose like a sugar loaf above the cotton plantations and the fields of maize.

Today these plantations are themselves only memories, and around the buried Sugar Loaf pyramid rises the elegant suburb of San Isidro, symbolic itself of all that can happen in Lima, a city where the destruction of monuments has always been common practice, and where ancient towns, fortresses, palaces, and churches have given way to incredibly ugly skyscrapers which manage to hide even the trim little two-storey Spanish colonial houses, with their brass or silver-studded doors and their airy cedar-wood balconies suspended over the crowded streets.

The plan to build a villa on top of the Sugar Loaf *Waka* was ambitious, but all that remains of this plan is the faint track spiralling up the sides. No powerful American car ever desecrated the sides of the *waka*, for before the road could be built countless mummies, crushed pottery, ancient fabrics, and jewels were discovered on the track, and a stop was put to this sacrilegious work. The owner's grandiose plans were at an end, for he could not face the dumb reproaches of the desecrated mummies, or the future visitations of the High Priestess whom we were later to see rising from the *waka*. Perhaps he was scared at the idea of the countless spirits whose homes would be devastated by his sacrilegious picks and shovels.

Only a few miles away from the Sugar Loaf there is another *waka* which actually does form the pedestal of a villa—which subsides a few inches each year, as the labyrinth of underground tunnels gives way.

There are innumerable strange and ghostly stories of what can happen to rash mortals who have the temerity to tamper with the dwelling-places of the mummies.

Under the blue skies of Lima, where the only humidity there is takes the form of a thick and irksome winter mist known as the *garua*, the centuries have greater respect than men for the precious fragments buried under the sands. Nevertheless, the voice of the scholar was at last heard above the din of the estate agent who was splitting up the great farms and plantations and tearing down the ruins dating from centuries before the Inca civilisation. The people began to show an interest in their great heritage.

The call to battle was sounded by the famous Peruvian archaeologist Julio Tello, shortly to be taken up by Dr. Arturo Jimenez-Borja, an expert on the earliest inhabitants of the Rimac valley. When we arrived his first task was already well under way, and the pre-Incan palace of Puruchucu, which stands on the lower slopes of the maritime Andes about eight miles from Peru, was rising again in its ancient splendour against its background of cotton plantations; but this time with a museum beside it where everyone could examine and admire the treasures saved from its ruins.

Our interest in this work, and our very first historical-archaeological adventures, date from the moment we saw this palace. What a fascinating apprenticeship it was, so full of unsolved problems and endowed with a slightly nightmarish quality arising from the necessity of living for so long in the strange half-world of the mummies. Our hands and eyes knew the feverish excitement of glimpsing a few sticks of bamboo or a shred of white cloth, which were the only visible signs of a burial ground, half hidden under the desert sand. We searched frantically, first for traces and then for the origins of these forgotten people, who, driven by their own internal schisms and by the Inca advance, had come down from the heights of the Andes to the shores of the Pacific, to the great empty desert, where the only features in its arid chalky soil were the gorges and ravines left by mountain torrents falling from their heights to be lost in the depths of the ocean.

How were we to set about finding something of the fantastic lives of these people who had lived so long before the Inca civilisation, and of whom so little was known today? Patient research, together with a close study of the scraps bearing witness to their daily occupations and their artistic pursuits, gave us more and more cause for astonishment. It was odd to think that we were living a mere stone's throw from that famous and long-neglected pyramid, on the very spot where they had built their city. It was a strange thought that below us mummies were sleeping, still prisoners of the sands until perhaps some great earthquake should come to release them and bury us in their place.

B

There were of course friends in plenty to warn us of the vengeance which the mummies would take on us, and which already threatened us in our dreams. Nor was this surprising, for in the first photographs we took of their pottery, woven materials and other objects dug out of the Sugar Loaf *Waka*, the prints showed everything extremely clearly except the mummies themselves. Where they should have been there was only a halo of light, and the archaeologist who was holding them up to be photographed was carefully cradling . . . nothing! Add to this the fact that both camera shutter and flashgun for a long time refused to function properly inside the *waka*, and our apprehension of the final results no longer seems so ludicrous.

These were not our only worries, for nothing seemed easy in our task of prehistorical reconstruction. We puzzled for days, for example, to find a suitable interpretation for the simple sketch executed by Huaman Poma, an Indian chronicler fascinated by the religious aspects of the Spanish conquest, showing the arrival in Lima of St. Bartholomew in an epoch when Pizarro and his companions regarded Peru as a golden land whose treasure should be removed along with its idolatory.

Archaeology, is still a very new study in Peru, in spite of the excellent work done by Tello, who, following in the steps of the Inca scholars or Amautas, was himself the leader of a band of Peruvian and foreign scholars, working together to try to throw some light on the origins and cultural significance of the early peoples and customs of Peru. One of the principal difficulties is to unravel the extent to which the various cultures were in close contact with each other, or rivals; did one culture lead on to the next, or were they merely sporadic outbursts, separated from the others by either space or time, or both? To help us in our search we had to call upon the resources not only of history and archaeology, but of linguistics, ethnology, paleomagnetism, archaeography, botany, carbon 14 dating, and symbolism.

Right from the start we were faced with problems. How, for

example, were we to interpret the name of Lima, our base? No
historical mention had been made of the source of the name since
Pizarro, four and a half centuries earlier, had traced out the hundred
and seventeen squares which were to make up the plan of the squares
and right-angled streets of this capital of the New Castille. The town
started as an oasis planted with pyramids, and was to become a
fairy-tale town, the greatest and most powerful of the New World,
from Panama and Quito to Chili and Buenos Aires, rustling with an
opulence worthy of the magnificent court of one of the richest
empires the world has ever seen.

Where were we to seek the origins of the mysterious Rimac, the
most favoured oracle of the valley aborigines, who spoke out her
wise prophecies from the depths of one of the pyramids, and gave
her name to both the river which still flows through Lima, and to the
valley itself? Alas, the legendary voice is no longer heard and no
trace of the oracle has ever been found.

Our task was further confused by the facts that the ancient yellow-
paged chronicles gave us only the vaguest of clues, and even then
these often contradicted one another. No interest at all appeared to
have been taken in pre-Inca civilisation since the very first Europeans
set foot on these shores. And, even if all the records of the *conquista-*
dores agree that the Incas conquered the province of Lima only a
short time before their own arrival, introducing their own language
(Quechua), it is nevertheless only too obvious that the Spaniards
found this same recently introduced language incredibly difficult to
understand, while the subtleties of the other surviving languages—
such as *aymara, uru-puquina, a'karo* or *kauki, mochica, yunga,* and
chinchaysuyo—made their task of unravelling the past an almost
impossible one.

The mosaic of different nations living on the Lima coast at the
time of the Spanish conquest is easily explained by the Inca method
of colonising new territories, which was to settle a loyal clan (a
group of families called a *mitimae*) in the recently conquered region,
and to marry the women to men who were their own loyal agents,

and who would in future control the territory for them. They also evolved a similar method for punishing recalcitrant tribes, but although this obviously worked successfully for the Incas, it did create a puzzling problem for future anthropologists who were to find northern races suddenly appearing in the south, or a clan of Pacific fishermen turning up on the shores of Lake Titicaca, over 12,000 feet above sea-level.

Indeed, our explorations into Peruvian prehistory were soon to bring us up against problems virtually insoluble at present for want of evidence, and until some future crumbling scrap of manuscript turns up to corroborate or overthrow our painfully acquired theories, we shall continue—like the Egyptologists before the discoveries of Champollion—to strive slowly to extend the frontiers of history by hypothesis. What is more, the further we went in our discoveries of these painted and embroidered materials, our studies of the decorated clay utensils, of objects used for domestic or ritual purposes, the tools and musical instruments which were to be our principal sources of information, the more firmly were we convinced that the pre-Inca peoples of the Pacific coast were neither backward in any way, nor savage races in perpetual conflict with each other. On the contrary we found proof of their commercial ties, not only with the nations on the high plateaux of the Andes, but also with the warlike tribes of the Amazon jungle.

In the same way we realised that although the earliest civilisations were strongly influenced by Andean cultures for many centuries, they later freed themselves from this influence and drew up their own individual codes of government and social life. Their religious rites were also modified to fit in with this new independence but they nevertheless retained their ancestors' belief in the importance of fecundity, the reliability of astrology, and the beneficial results of sacrifice. Allied to all this was a strong faith in the divine qualities of snakes, jaguars, llamas, dogs, monkeys; fish and shellfish, seaweed and shells; the pelican, certain kinds of owl, condors and parrots; spiders, scorpions, lizards, frogs, toads and salamanders, octopuses and squids; all these, together with the mountains and certain vegetables, made up the outlines of a magic 'map' by which Peruvians have been guided since the beginnings of their civilisation, and which still holds sway in the minds of those who dwell in the forests and mountains. Although these influences may be waning among the inhabitants of the busy towns, the same age-old symbols are to be found even in the centres of modern civilisation, decorating the *ponchos* and caps of modern Indian men, while the women carry the same motifs on their belts and purses and even their cooking-pots.

Naturally the continued contacts of so many maritime races was bound to lead to the cross-breeding of their cultures. Thus the first potters and painters of Lima were greatly inspired by the expressive art of the northern Mochica-Chimu, whose 'ladder' sign—symbol of the magic staircase leading from earth to heaven—features largely in the art of the ancient stone age civilisations of Tiahuanaco, together with an occasional vestige from the Chavin epoch (earliest of all the Peruvian civilisations) and several of the demoniacal fantasies of the Nazcas and Paracas.

We were thus able to make out a current of shared traditions which to our knowledge had hardly been remarked upon before, and which had its roots in the ancient days of the Perunruna—the desert people—about whom Huaman Poma said that they were 'countless as the sand, and so wise that their wives never practised adultery'.

These traditions were revealed by the recent archaeological discoveries which led Kroeber to announce in 1944 that 'all the aboriginal civilisations of Peru made up a unity, a historical whole ... a deep cultural stream ...', thus repudiating the popular misconception that the whole of the pre-Columbian era was one of permanent strife and discord, with each small nation continually at war with its neighbour.

The three geographical regions of the country—coast, Andes, and Amazon—shared a great many common traditions, of which the evidence can be found in the similarity of the clothes in the different regions, an analogous worship of ancestral mummies, the identical use of idols, oracles, and divinities, comparable astronomical knowledge, similar architectural forms, textile, metallurgical, and ceramic arts employing the same raw materials, the worship of mountain peaks or of the pyramids which were built up in their image, the veneration of any strange phenomenon of nature, the same religious organisation centring around their pyramids, great numbers of priests and priestesses subjected to the strictest of discipline, ritual bathing and confession, and by a way of communal life and work directed largely towards the benefit of the society as a whole, and moved by a meticulous sense of justice.

It is easy to see why, with all the doubts and mysteries which still exist, no one had attempted to fill in the picture sketched by numerous legends over the centuries of the first inhabitants of Lima. It is only now, thanks largely to the excavations of Dr. Jimenez-Borja at which we were present, that we have been able to penetrate their hitherto unknown world.

It was not without considerable emotion that we first lifted the masks from the faces of these mummies resurrected from the sands. The masks were made of wood or blood-coloured linen, painted in blue or gold, the great staring eyes with their pitchy pupils gazing out from countless years of silence which had never before been broken.

II

THE PRE-INCAS OF LIMA

More and more archaeological discoveries were coming to light in the Rimac valley more or less on Lima's doorstep, and we followed these finds with growing interest. At Lurin, to the south of the capital, we saw uncovered the foundations of an extraordinary building surrounding an enormous buried chapel, in which we were to find, hidden among the pieces of black pottery, a scrap of grey-brown material woven with a design of pyramids in yellow and blue.

It was at Paracas that we saw our first mummy lifted from its *fardo*—a cocoon of burial garments containing the mummified figure, together with objects precious to it in its lifetime. Paracas is known throughout the world for the embroidered materials which swathe the bodies of its noble ancestors, sitting in their baskets in the depths of monumental caverns or burial chambers. From these burial chambers (which were often made in the form of a bottle, containing families or even clans) our learned friend Tello was later to unearth, in less than a month, as many as 429 mummies piled high one upon the other.

At Infantas, to the north of Lima, we found a tiny stopper lying among the great heaps of whitened skulls on the site of an opened pyramid; it was carved in wood in the shape of a monkey, and there was also a mummified hand tattooed with red, its index finger raised as if to advert us of some imminent catastrophe.

Even further to the north, at Chancay, we came upon a deep layer of pottery objects contained in tall egg-shaped earthenware jars, not one of them broken or cracked and all looking as if they had been set down on their bed of sand only the previous day. From there we brought back one of these little statues called *cochimilcos*—a little sacred doll made of clay with an upturned pointed nose, its hands and eyes raised as if to beg a favour from the gods.

Then came an extraordinary discovery which, had it occurred in ancient Egypt, would have taken the whole world by storm; happening as it did in Peru hardly anyone outside Lima heard about it at all, so little interest have the Peruvians in even the rarest relics of their past. At the elegant suburb of San Isidro the mummified body of a woman had been found, who was the proud owner of what no other beauty in the world—not Cleopatra, nor the Mona Lisa, nor even Venus de Milo—had ever possessed: hair more than seven feet long! (see plate XVI).

The citizens of Lima fell for this age-old beauty who crouched on her finely woven mat of russet-coloured rushes, her chin resting on a slender artistic hand, the wrist encircled by a blackened silver bangle, while the thick tresses of her dark brown hair spread like a cloak around her. She seemed to be observing the people who surrounded her, as curious to know about us as we were to find out about her, and a slight smile touched her lips as if she was just about to tell us what it had been like to carry around such a superb mane of hair.

It was hard to imagine the owner of such hair (floating behind her like the tail of some swiftly moving comet) bothering about everyday tasks, when everything about her, her dress, and her ornaments, seemed to point to her being a person of high degree. For us she became the 'High Priestess' of the Sugar Loaf Pyramid, retaining her title even after our archaeologist friend, amused by our enthusiasm, had gently pointed out that our Vestal Virgin was equipped with a sewing-box which, although a very pretty one, was proof that she had practised the arts of weaving, embroidering, and even mending just like the other girls of the time.

Her name? That we would never know. Her age? About twenty-five. How could we find out more about our strange neighbour? What race of people was it who had buried her with such care in this ancient tomb? We felt a great urge to give back a fleeting moment of life to this beautiful maiden by finding out something of her history.

★   ★   ★

It was Dr. Jimenez-Borja who gave us our first clue to the High Priestess's tribe and history. 'It's something to do with the Wallas,' he informed us laconically, bringing us in proof of this theory a paper written in June 1942, by Dr. Julio Tello. This informed us that the Sugar Loaf Pyramid or *waka* was part of an archaeological group called the Walla-Marka, in which were included other pyramids called Juliana, Lima Tambo, and Santa Beatriz. It also maintained that the Sugar Loaf was one of the most important pyramids in the Lima valley, because one of the many tombs (which were piled high on top of each other inside it) is known to be extremely old, being made up of conical lumps of rough brick piled up to look either like the ears of Indian corn—a very different formation from those found in all the other pyramids of the valley.

We quickly seized a map of the area and were able to locate several place-names between the Sugar Loaf and the nearby Andes, which, in spite of the variations to be found in their modern spelling, were nevertheless extremely significant in their oldest forms: Huachi-Walla, Kara-Walla (or Carabayllo), Wadka-Walla— remnants of settlements built by this race towards the end of its long migration from the Andean heights to the Pacific coast.

Eager to trace the journey of the Wallas right back to its source, we spread out a map of the whole of Peru and poured over it till dawn. Our curiosity was repaid, and the map began to give up its secrets. Their route appeared to lead us from the heart of Lima itself, through the outskirts and up the steep narrow gulleys of the Andes across the icy plateaux and the arid windswept Pampas plains with their blanket of thick cloud, twisting and turning through glaciers and volcanoes until it gradually descended through valleys suddenly green with thick forests and cut by hidden rivers, leading us eventually to the legendary Cuzco, ancient capital of that mysterious Manco, founder of the Inca empire. Yes, surely this was the way the Wallas had come to Lima—by none other than the famous Inca road, the Nan Cuna or 'Road of Time', which was probably in its day the best road in the world.

But when we poured out our theory to Dr. Jimenez-Borja, it did not receive quite the reaction we had expected. We had, of course, realised that our new theories might cause a storm among historians more experienced than ourselves. What were we going to do? Were we going to tear up all we had so patiently written on the subject? Which of our critics could be sure that our thesis, built up on innumerable minute facts and figures from these bygone days, was not just as good if not better than anything they could do themselves?

Dr. Jimenez-Borja listened to our problem with a smile, before confirming that all those who had done research into the pre-Columbian era admitted in general that the many tribes who inhabited the Lima valley before the Incas did seem to have a definite family relationship, and that this was perhaps because they shared common roots in the Aymara culture. He went on to tell us of certain suburbs of Lima whose names had clearly come from the Aymara tongue: Chucuito, Huancane, Copacabana, Callao—all these were names of towns or villages on the shores of Lake Titicaca, 12,000 feet above sea-level, where thousands of fishermen, farmers, weavers, and shepherds live today exactly as they did in the time of the ancient Aymara civilisation. What could possibly account for these same names being found both at the sacred lake of the early Peruvians and on the shores of the Pacific—districts at least a thousand miles apart, separated by the wildest and most savage countryside? Even if no one knows the final answer, we can be sure that those who first

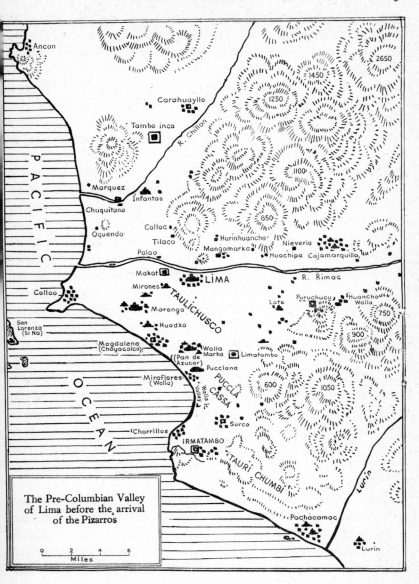

The Pre-Columbian Valley
of Lima before the arrival
of the Pizarros

0   2   4   6
Miles

descended from the heights were faced by one of the most epic journeys of all time.

There seemed to be only one definite historical fact: the Rimac valley had known two great cultures: the pre-Inca of which very little is known, and the other, generally attributed to the famous Parachutec—who in the fifteenth century conquered the peoples living along the Pacific shore. But no one knew whether these peoples had originally come there as serious colonisers, or because of that peculiar atavistic element of character which makes the Peruvian Indian a perpetual nomad always ready to move on, his bundle on his back and his traditions and beliefs in his head. A man who is always different in hair-style and dress from all other races and tribes, he at all times takes with him his own tongue and the undying memory of his birthplace, the name of which he transfers to his new country.

Without really knowing whether the Walla epic had been the outcome of a panic-stricken flight or of what one might call secular tourism, we were just preparing to follow them along the Lima-Cuzco road when our friend Jimenez-Borja suddenly arrived triumphantly waving a ragged fragment of paper. This was the document we had been looking for without any success for the past six months: an article written by Carlos Romero, a former director of the Lima National Library. It contained the family tree of the Wallas of Lima taken directly from one of their last descendants, a man called Timoran who lived in La Magdalena—the district which was originally called Chayacalca, where the Pucla Cassa palace belonging to the Walla Regulo was found by the Spanish *conquistadores*.

Carlos Romero had worked for many years with the famous German archaeologist Max Uhle, known as the father of Peruvian archaeology. They had done a great deal of excavation in the Rimac valley, and he was a firm believer in the tremendous importance of the ancient civilisations which had flourished there and which had been suddenly brought to light by the discovery in one of the pyramids of an underground tunnel leading into a 'sacred village', believed to have been built by the Wallas, and still to be seen in Lima today.

Men have lived in the Rimac valley from the very earliest times, as can be seen from the great heaps of remains still to be explored. These lead us to deduce that the valley has been inhabited for count-less centuries, but it is not possible to say when or from where the people came. It has been maintained that the people who lived in this valley belonged to a race of fishermen who also lived on the nearby coast to the north and south of Callao (Lima's harbour).

These fishermen of ancient Peru were recently placed in the 'pre-ceramic age' by Dr. Frederick Engel, although he added that they were not in the least primitive, for their technical skill was much more advanced than anyone had hitherto realised, and he concluded that their civilisation was comparable to that of Egypt before the Pharaohs.

However, our most useful information on the chronology of the pre-Columbian era came from Vilar-Cordova's book on the subject. This author continually stresses that it is very hard to have any accurate information about the chronology of this time, for unlike the Mayas these people had no calendar nor, as far as we know, any form of hieroglyphic writing. These prehistoric fishermen lived on what they caught from the sea, and found shelter in little huts near the coast. The remains of what they used to eat has formed thick layers of a shell-like substance often ten to fifteen feet deep, in which one can find empty shells and sometimes fish bones or crudely polished stone knives.

It is possible to trace the transition from a civilisation based solely on fishing to one which combined fishing and agriculture: the layers of remains mark the change by their contents of 'archaeological' vegetables, among which can be found kidney beans, cotton seeds, peanuts, guava seeds, the stones of several other fruits, and empty gourds. The higher layers reveal the beginning of cooking and weaving, and we find fragments of loosely woven material together with the charred remains of gourd cooking-pots, and the shattered morsels of oxidised stone with which they heated their water in bark containers. Next there are signs that we have reached the beginning of the Proto-Lima civilisation, when the agricultural tribes became extraordinarily talented in weaving, pottery, painting, and embroidery—arts which were carried on in the *markas* or communal villages built round their central pyramids which were used by later generations as temples and burial grounds.

It was in this period that the first signs were seen of the influence of the Mochica-Chimu people from the north, and of the southern Nazca-Paracas, and, later on, traces of the famous Tiahuanaco civilisation bring us gradually up to the time of the Inca conquest itself. According to Dr. Carlos Romero, in the second half of the thirteenth century an Aymara race called the Wallas, one of those which had created the Tiahuanaco civilisation, came from their own distant lands and settled along one side of this valley; their chieftain was a man called Puglia. At the time of the Spanish conquest the district between Barranco and La Magdalena was still called the Walla Valley, while in the Miraflores quarter there was a village also called Walla. Near by there was an enormous pyramid called Pugliana, a name which the Spaniards changed to Juliana, and the chief ruling at the time was called Puglia Cassa. So we are already familiar with the Inca custom of calling chieftains by the names of their tribes, and as we know that that particular 'Walla' pyramid dates back to a very early period, we are entitled to say that the Wallas living in Lima at the time were almost certainly the ones who had emigrated from Cuzco.

You can imagine how delighted we were to find our theory corroborated by one of the greatest Peruvian historians even if we were not the first to make the Wallas the original inhabitants of Cuzco and then of Lima.

It was Carlos Romero's article which persuaded us to continue our study of the Lima valley. From him we learned that there had been another migration later—also Aymara, but this time most probably from Callao (a high plateau near Lake Titicaca) which came down the Huarochiri gorge and settled all the way along the foothills of the Lima valley, on the surrounding hills, and on the land near the coast. We learned that these people were called the Huanchos from Jimenez-Borja, who had found the mummified figure of one of their noblemen among the ruins of the Puruchuco Palace, together with some particularly fine *kipus* (see Glossary). Thus the valley which the Incas found on their arrival was like another Babylon, and everywhere they went they found settled towns.

If it is true that the conquest of the Peruvian coast was carried out under the orders of the great Inca ruler, Pachacutec the Reformer (as is recorded in the tales told by the Amauta and Kipukamayok tribes, and taken down by the Spanish chroniclers), then it must have been during the reign of Huayna Kapak that the Incas arrived at the gates of Lima. The ruler of the province at that time was the mighty *kuraka* (local chief) Kassa-Pajsi, whose residence was in the Chayacala (Magdalena) district. Of course, it must be remembered that in those days Lima was probably only one of the villages making up the great Cuismancu kingdom which is mentioned by so many chroniclers, particularly the half-caste writer Garcilaso de la Vega Inca.

The identity of Cuismancu is yet another enigma. Some historians go so far as to deny his existence altogether, while others hail him as one of the great chieftains of the Mochica era.

Garcilaso has much more positive information. Cuismancu, he tells us, ruled over the Rimac valley and all the surrounding valleys, stretching from the Barranca river to the north of the capital as far as the Mala river in the south. These valleys together with the nearby gorges were placed under the protection of Irma, the powerful goddess of that coast whose place was soon to be usurped by another god—equally invisible—the all-powerful Pachacaman.

Cuismancu was king, judge, and priest to the coast-dwelling Yungas. These people lived in a theocratic community typical of the pre-Inca civilisations along the coast in which the aim was to promote peaceful work which would make everyone as happy as possible. In these communities agriculture was developed to such an extent that, having reclaimed waste ground on the borders of the desert, tens of thousands of people were able to live off the land. This seems reasonably certain, for countless vestiges have been found of irrigation works, towns, crumbling pyramids, burial grounds, and mummies.

Cuismancu is said to have been addicted to the arts of soothsaying and magic, and believed himself able to speak with invisible spirits and interpret their wishes. Before the arrival of the Incas he ruled over the people called Limacs or Rimacs, and had allied himself with his powerful neighbour Chuquismancu, ruler of Huarco-Mala as well as the great Chimu or leader of the Chinchas. But when Cuismancu sallied forth at the head of 30,000 warriors to defend his kingdom against the Incas a most extraordinary thing happened: the famous general Kapak Yupanki, who was brother of the Inca chieftain Pachacutec, was so impressed by the spiritual development of his enemies that—although he had come all the way to the border of the Yunga kingdom in order to fight them—he actually offered Cuismancu not, as might have been expected, terms of honourable surrender, but an actual treaty of alliance.

PLATE I

Puccla, just as he was when dug out of one of the terraces of the Sugar Loaf *Waka*. This Walla chieftain is reputed to have worn a belt stuffed with coca leaves and magic seeds.

You can imagine Cuismancu's surprise on hearing the Inca emissary's unexpected proposal that they should not begin to fight until they had met to discuss their religion and their gods; that there was no reason why they should not be friends and brothers instead of enemies; that the Inca kings were willing in the future to worship the Rimac god as well as their own Pachacamac, provided that the Rimac people would also worship the sun. And it was thus that they exchanged their gods, and Cuismancu and the neighbouring rulers stayed in their own kingdoms, and the Incas esteemed and worshipped the Oracle of Rimac and ordered all their people to do likewise.

PLATE II

The funeral *fardos* of Chinita and Puccla. Innumerable coils of hand-woven white cotton were wound around the crouching figure of the mummy, and then sewn down one side before being crowned with a false head.

C

III

WALLA-MARKA, AN OASIS IN THE DESERT

Among the first inhabitants of the Rimac valley to rise before us from the desert sands (together with the belongings which were to give us so many clues to their beliefs, occupations, arts, and amusements) were the people who had lived around the Sugar Loaf Pyramid in the village of Walla-Marka.

The strange thing is that the desert which surrounds the valley, with its gently rolling hills of brownish-yellow sand, is surprisingly similar to the lonely heights of the Aymara plateaux, for the coastal desert is as barren as the high steppes, and the ocean as impressively calm as that enormous lake (Titicaca) which lies among the topmost peaks of the Andes.

We can imagine how surprised Puccla must have been when, having left the dramatic heights and led his men along the side of a chasm down an interminably long and winding gully, he caught a glimpse between the rocks of endless pale-yellow sands bordered by the green line of the waves, with that immense blue pool of mingled sea and sky superimposed, which men were later to call the Pacific.

Puccla and his people may well have been cheered on their journey by the little bushes and cacti springing from the barren rocks, and the softer air and gentler breezes of the lower slopes must have made their long and arduous trek seem worth while in spite of the hazards and privations of the journey. Did they have to fight to stay there? We know nothing of what happened to them before the arrival of the Incas; the silence surrounding them is broken only by the voice of the famous oracle of Rimac making her pact with the Inca Sun God, after which it encircles them again until the arrival of Pizarro and the Spanish *conquistadores*.

It is the history of this lost period of time that we were attempting to unravel by making our slow way up the terraced sides of the Walla-Marka Pyramid.

On our first day of excavations, however, the Wallas' pyramid seemed little more than a sandy hillock. A tangled mass of greenery covered the base, and the summit—although more than sixty feet high—was almost entirely hidden by a curtain of giant eucalyptus trees.

The task of restoring the monument was further complicated by a tenacious growth of pink and mauve bougainvilias planted as a decoration by the gardener who had lived at the foot of the *waka*. In fact, these bougainvilias caused rather a dramatic scene: Jimenez-Borja, always precise and methodical in everything he did, had fixed a date for the clearing of the hill to be finished. On the evening before this date the workmen had decided to sprinkle the flowers with petrol and set fire to them in order to speed up the work. There was nothing wrong with this plan, except that the flames quickly spread up the sides of the pyramid, and no water could be used to extinguish them in case it penetrated to the funeral chambers and harmed the mummies. You may be sure that not a word of this was told to Jimenez-Borja when he was shown the cleared site the next day by a group of pale and trembling navvies; nor did he learn, until later, that he himself had narrowly missed being roasted alive, together with his precious mummies, when the fire suddenly flared up again in the middle of the night. It was the owners of the luxury villas surrounding the pyramid who called the fire brigade, thus averting a catastrophe which they were perfectly sure was the direct result of tampering with the mummies.

Naturally enough all the work to be done on the site—the clearing, washing, and piecing together of fragments—was a costly business. As our pyramid rose gradually from the engulfing sands we began to see it differed in structure and substance from the other *wakas* in the valley. Did this mean that it was the oldest of all the pre-Inca monuments? Certainly it was one of the most ancient—much older than the mummies and their possessions which were buried in it. We were thus dealing with what were called 'intruder tombs', a name given to a place of burial which had originally been used as a place of worship, before being made into a sepulchre. And indeed, as the excavations grew deeper, we were able to perceive a succession of different civilisations, each of which had left its priceless legacy behind.

But which of the ancient tribes had actually built the Walla-Marka? Was it the same people who had covered the desert with pyramids of all sizes, sometimes singly, sometimes in groups of more than sixty? These could be found all over, from Chincha on the south Pacific coast right up to Piura in the very north of Peru, but whether the Sugar Loaf was one of their number was something we did not yet know.

One fact which emerged quite clearly, however, was that the original builders of the pyramid had not used it as a sepulchre. This supported the theory of a large number of scholars that the *wakas* had been intended originally not as tombs but as temples. Indeed, we ourselves had found nothing in the deeper layers of these pyramids but broken pieces of pottery unaccompanied by a single corpse. It was of course possible that later comers might have disposed of the bodies, and this theory was supported by the fact that the method of burying people wrapped up in a bundle with their belongings was not practised along the Peruvian coast until much later on. But when we were later shown some bones which workmen had found lying outside with some fragments of pottery dating back to the Chavin civilisation (the earliest known of them all), the very antiquity of the pottery pointed to the skeletons belonging to some unknown tribe who had built the *waka* as a temple and buried their people round about.

Also we do know that the inhabitants of the north of Peru used to

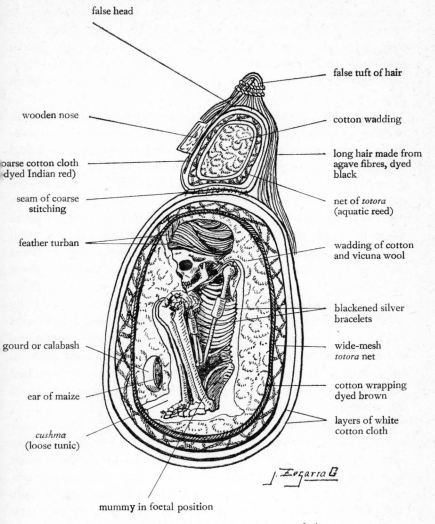

false head

false tuft of hair

wooden nose

cotton wadding

coarse cotton cloth
(dyed Indian red)

long hair made from
agave fibres, dyed
black

seam of coarse
stitching

net of *totora*
(aquatic reed)

feather turban

wadding of cotton
and vicuna wool

blackened silver
bracelets

wide-mesh
totora net

gourd or calabash

cotton wrapping
dyed brown

ear of maize

layers of white
cotton cloth

cushma
(loose tunic)

mummy in foetal position

SECTION OF A TYPICAL WALLA-MARKA *fardo*
WITH ITS FALSE HEAD

The sketch shows the contents and the bindings used by the ancient
Peruvians of the Pacific coast.

bury their dead beneath the sand after laying them out on litters of woven reeds which they called *barbacoas*. As they buried them with very little clothing on, however, they did not remain nearly so well preserved as the swaddled corpses of Lima and Paracas; the fact that we found any trace of them at all was only thanks to the miraculous preserving power of the sand.

The custom of swaddling the dead in funeral cloths or *fardos* seems to have been brought in by immigrants from the south. An enormous number of well-preserved *fardos* have been found in the burial grounds of Paracas, the deserts of the Nazca, and the plains of Ica. Presumably this style of burial later extended over the whole of Peru during the astonishingly fast spread of the Tiahuanaco culture. The order of the layers which we found in our pyramid supported this: all the mummies in the Sugar Loaf had been buried fully dressed in all their finery, masked and turbanned to such an extent that they rose before our eyes like ghostly life-size dolls resting in their own silent world, some just under the surface of the earth and some several feet lower. They had settled themselves down for eternity in little holes filled with offerings and sand, singly or in pairs, or even several piled one on top of the other; some were laid out in rows in actual funeral chambers built of *adobe* bricks, and covered with a roof made of bamboo and caked earth which was held up by thorny branches; occasionally we found them in the depths of a stone-tiled well shaped like a bottle.

After a year of untiring work one whole side and a corner of the pyramid were restored to show three terraced steps, each one narrower than the one below, sloping steeply up to the summit which could itself be reached by about fifty steps. With our boots, clothing, hair, eyebrows, and lashes whitened by the ancient sandy dust of the excavations, we made our way up to the top, just a little stunned by what we were seeing. Napoleon's soldiers had contemplated centuries from the top of the Egyptian pyramids, but how many centuries lay before our eyes? Problems of dates and details of the prehistoric tribes who had lived along these shores faded from our minds in front of this delightful panorama. Beyond the rooftops of the elegant villas, dominated by the domes of the white Spanish-style churches, the town of Lima lay displayed before us—a city half-colonial, half ultra-modern in style—with its skyscrapers lifting their ugly necks to the sky, overshadowing the older districts and even dominating the great avenues, whose enormous lighted street signs outrival by night the lights of many a greater city. The thickly inhabited districts stretch out as far as the first slopes of the Andes, which are dotted with their tumbledown shanties, while every day a little more land from the great cotton estates is nibbled away by the residential or industrial suburbs. On the horizon the great barrier of violet and bronze mountains pierces the sky, quite bare of any sort of vegetation, crumpled and contorted.

Unmoving, vast, and nearly always veiled in grey mists, the ocean gazes at this fantastic panorama, while its dull monotonous roar forms a permanent backcloth to the people of the coast. From time to time there are dramatic submarine upheavals and little rocky islands emerge from the water, black and smooth as sharks' fins. In time their tips become whitened by guano. Larger and more grey, the island of San Fernando stands facing Callao; now a prison island, it was in bygone days the Si Na of the Mochica tribes, and remained the temple in which they practised their worship of a lunar god in their almost lunar landscape.

It is impossible to imagine a people, no matter how long ago they lived, who would not be profoundly influenced by this great pale-washed backcloth, its edges softened by desert sand and mist, full of whispering murmurs but never troubled by any ungodly din. The only voices raised above the ordinary march of human life would have been the auguries of the mysterious oracle of Rimac, the *kuraka* addressing his people, the magi's prayers, or the screams of the sacrificial victims at the hour when the engraved silver bowl was offered to the gods, full of blood or *chica* (an intoxicating drink).

We might have heard the squeaking of the ploughman's sandals as he tilled the ground with his primitive wooden tool, or the cries of thousands of sea-birds skimming along the shore in an endless swerving maze. Or again, at the moment when the Andes blaze like a glowing cinder lit up by the last rays of the sun dying in amethyst splendour into the ocean, we might have heard the faint notes of a flute, fashioned from the bone of a llama, in whose music, straying beneath the finger of a sand-blinded musician, is captured the whole essence of the desert scene. At the same time the penetrating melody played on the little pottery pipes seems to find an answer in the faraway faint tinkle of the tiny bells made of gold, silver, or copper hanging from the litter which (studded with precious stones) was used to carry the ruler to and from his palace of sun-baked mud.

Little bells, pipes of Pan, flutes, sandals, farming tools, silver vases so finely beaten that not one of the famous silversmiths of Lima would even attempt to beat out the dents, masks of the magi, of the *kuraka*, of the High Priestess, all these were restored to our fascinated eyes as day by day we uncovered them with trembling and careful hands. All that was missing was the voice of the oracle, silent now for ever, and the sight of those mummies whom the violation of past centuries had robbed from our eyes.

★   ★   ★

The High Priestess (see plate XVI) was nothing more at first than a shell of white cloth (the *fardo*) topped by a mask made of reddened cloth stuffed with cotton, which had been completely flattened by the heavy weight of sand on top of it, so that the wooden nose had fallen off and the mask itself, crowned by a chignon of false hair, had almost been torn from its base. Her neighbour rose soon after her from the tomb, swathed in countless yards of white material and crowned with the most extraordinary cloth, the mask representing an Asiatic type of face covered with horizontal red and blue tattoo marks. It was such a realistic-looking mask with its round eyes, its long wooden nose, and its fringed wig of short straight hair, that the native workmen were reluctant to touch this pretty little Chinese

girl, or 'Chinita' as they christened her. Was she perhaps the descendant of the legendary and beautiful Llira who was said to have come
from Asia after the great flood? Or perhaps a relation of the gracious
Ceterni, the favourite of the mysterious king Naymlamp, who had
arrived aboard a vessel of balsa wood bearing idols of emerald and
jade, and accompanied by an ostentatious number of courtiers who
had settled down all along the coast? No one could guess her origin,
and she will remain a beautiful enigma for ever.

The Magus was just as strange a figure, with his thin little mouth
made out of a strip of metal, and round beady eyes which gave him
a slightly frightened expression.

Then there was the mummy with the little squint wooden nose,
wild black hair streaked with white, and a mouth set in a fiendish
grin like some diabolical Jack-in-the-box, possibly a sorceress. The
name stuck, and sorceress she remained both in name and aspect,
with her great orange-feathered turban trembling in the slightest
breeze and her cheeks puffed out as if to utter a magic spell.

The next one to arrive on the stage was the most striking of all
and we immediately called him Puccla (see Chapter I). The mocking
face peered out from under a crimson turban; his chin was pointed
and the black pupils looked out in joyful surprise from the round
white eyes, carefully muffled in a white scarf; the two pouches
hanging from his belt were stuffed with *coca* and his tubular belt
bulged with magic seeds; he seemed to be coming forward like a
good prince to welcome us to the kingdom of the Walla-Marka.
In spite of his grand and dignified appearance he and his silent
entourage soon became our inseparable friends; such care had gone
into dressing them and into the making of their burial garments
that they all seemed ready to start on a new life instead of having
just finished with life.

The astonishing thing was the number of mummies who were to
be reborn in this way from our Sugar Loaf Pyramid. By the end of
eight months we had seen more than five hundred of them and they
seemed as surprised to see us as we were to see them. Besides the

A FUNERAL CHAMBER IN THE SUGAR LOAF *Waka*

This chamber contained two fardos with mummies, of which only one bore a false head. There were also several oars, and a number of earthenware pots. The sketch shows traces of the bamboo roof, and the maize-shaped adobe which is typical of this particular *waka*. The height of the chamber is 7 ft. 6 ins.

actual figures, we counted more than a thousand skulls which we later burnt on the vast bonfire which blazed on the summit of the pyramid—a last sacrifice which, though it may have surprised the ancient gods, was preferable to the state in which we had found other ancient sites, where failure to tidy up the remains had meant that the mummified skulls were used as playthings by the children of the district, who also robbed the tombs of anything of value. It was unlikely that the children could attempt to justify their actions by citing the precedent of their Inca ancestors, who used to drink from the skulls of their captured enemies:

> We shall drink from the traitor's skull,
> his teeth shall be our necklace,
> flutes shall be made from his bones,
> and we shall dance to the rhythm of the drums
> which we make from his skin.

It can be seen that these tombs are real archaeological gems, containing not only the mummified figures of an ancient and almost unknown civilisation, but the objects apparently held in highest esteem by the people themselves seem to be irrefutable proof of the artistic achievements of this civilisation.

The Wallas have at last risen from oblivion, to prove themselves as worthy of interest as the Incas, the Chimus, or the Nazcas. Let us to the best of our ability endeavour to outline their story, which has been so long concealed by the centuries.

IV

ENCYCLOPEDIA OF THE SANDS

A Peruvian archaeologist has said that the most valuable and complete of all the natural museums is to be found in the stretch of desert sand running alongside the Pacific.

Indeed, 'museum' does seem to be the most apt name for this South American Sahara, yielding as it does layer after layer of piled-up treasures from all the pre-Columbian civilisations. It could also be called the encyclopedia of the sands, and nowhere could you find a better-informed work of reference, more copiously illustrated than any book on art, history, or any of the sciences—provided, of course, that you can read.

We must admit that when we first went into this desert museum —where the characters are remarkably lifelike and show themselves to have been extraordinarily energetic and industrious— when we first opened this encyclopedia which dealt with their prehistory, we felt rather like schoolboys on their very first day at school.

One of the first things which surprises any apprentice in archaeology is to see his tutor eagerly pick up, clean, measure, and label the tiniest little piece of broken pottery as if it were the most expensive diamond you could find; and then to see during the very first lesson how that insignificant fragment of pottery, which he would previously have scraped off his boots without noticing its existence, suddenly become a clue of the utmost value. The detective and the archaeologist have much in common. The archaeologist has to devote much patience, time, and energy to meticulous searching and enquiry into a period which very often has no known history at all, where a tiny fragment of broken pottery can tell him all about the man who made it, his race, when and where he lived.

Let us then open the great natural encyclopedia which tells us about the Wallas, with the same wonderment and enquiry as a child who observes the kaleidoscope of new life around him on a spring day. Our encyclopedia is a strange book made up of sand and of clay, of scraps of linen, bamboo, and wood, of great gourds, a little precious metal, a great deal of patience and hard work.

As we leant over the trench cut to a depth of about ten feet along the side of the Sugar Loaf we wondered what we were going to see. Around us the Indian workmen tapped the ground gently with the points of their picks and mattocks, unearthing lumps of yellowed cotton, tufts of brownish llama wool, pieces of cloth and frayed tapestry, all of which were put on one side to be studied and classified later.

The centre of the pyramid was made up of this mixture of sand and fragments of material. It was not impossible, however, that there might be a funeral chamber beneath all this mess—the burial place of some great person, which might contain a wealth of valuable information.

The platforms were built round a central embankment, each platform covered with the mummies' cells, all made of the familiar *adobe* tooth-shaped bricks which suggested a Chavinoid influence. Now if we take Bennet's chronology as our guide, we find that the Chavinoid culture began about 1200 B.C. and went on until A.D. 400. We can therefore deduce that the Walla-Marka pyramid was built as a place of worship by a primitive race of people, who gave way to a race which attached great importance to the smallest piece of cultivatable ground because it had learnt the arts of agriculture and used the former temples as depositories for their mummies.

As the excavations proceeded, the newly revealed layers provided us with a great deal of information through the various types of pottery, which provide modern archaeology with one of its most valuable keys.

The first and therefore most recent pottery to appear were the Chancay *wakos*, or ceremonial dishes, recognisable by the cream colour, the rough texture of their surface, and their ornamentation of geometrical designs crudely sketched in a brown so dark as to be almost black. There was little of this type of pottery to be found at the Walla-Marka, and although not very old (Bennet gives the date of the Chancay culture as A.D. 1300 to 1438), it was clearly of a much lower standard than the pottery made during the previous century in the north and south of the country.

The next layer revealed the Tiahuanaco ceremonial dishes, which were more delicate, had a smoother finish, and were painted in red, black, and white; these dated from A.D. 1000 to 1300, and were accompanied by dishes in brick colour without any ornamentation.

Lower down we found the almost black Maranga pottery which was made between A.D. 400 and 1000, the period said to be the greatest of all for the quality and decoration in pottery making, and among it a Chincha ceremonial dish, probably brought as a present by some rich visitor coming from the southern deserts.

Thus, taken together, the different layers formed a sample of the cultural evolution which began somewhere around the fifth century, to be rudely interrupted in 1532 by Pizarro and his *conquistadores*.

But two mysteries still remained to be solved: what had happened around the Sugar Loaf *Waka* in the epoch following the Chancay culture, when the first Incas arrived from Cuzco in the Rimac valley? Why was there no trace of the well-known Inca pottery in the uppermost layers of the excavation? Or even a sign of its influence, as had occasionally been found elsewhere? Acting on the theory that the Inca tombs might have been broken up and scattered when preparations for the famous villa on the pyramid were going forward, many long hours were spent searching around the base among the bones and other rubbish, without finding anything at all worthy of note.

The second unsolved mystery was whether when we had dug right down to the base or lowest platform we would find any proof of a Chavinoid occupation to confirm Dr. Tello's assumption, already backed up by the shape of the *adobe* bricks used in parts of the pyramid's construction. Opinions were sharply divided on this point: some thought we would find nothing in the foundations of the *waka* because its first function had been that of a temple, not of a burial chamber; others were convinced that here (as in Egypt) the pyramids had since their beginning been both tombs and a means of linking the world of men with the world of the gods.

Even if the building material was different from Egypt (unbaked brick instead of stone), and although our pyramid had never reached the same height as the Egyptian ones (though there is evidence to show that it had once been much higher than at present), we could not help comparing it with the 4,700-year-old Sakkarat, most ancient of all the Egyptian pyramids.

Perhaps the ancient Peruvian tribes felt as proud as the earliest Egyptians to have found a form of monument where, as Samivel describes it, 'the marriage of heaven and earth finds its consummation'. We could not help feeling that in both Egypt and Peru the tombs were a *result* of the pyramids having been built rather than the *reason* for building them. Would we really find proof of a Chavinoid settlement, men who had come down from the mysterious Chavin de Huantar, more than 12,500 feet up in the Cordillera Blanca to the north of Lima?

At our present stage in the excavations, however, we had to content ourselves with placing the Sugar Loaf *Waka* against the background of pre-Tiahuanaco culture, which seemed to suit it best.

*   *   *

Our encyclopedia of the sands was illustrated by samples of pottery, whose variation in design and technique illustrated the successive waves of people who had arrived over the centuries, from the high

Aymara plateaux, the mountains round Cuzco, the northern peaks, or the southern deserts to settle along the Lima coast. All the evidence we possess leads us to believe that the Wallas were a friendly peace-loving people, working hard and living happily in their moderate climate.

This climate must certainly have surprised them, and one wonders how long it took to adapt themselves to life at sea-level. Nevertheless, once settled in the green oasis of the Rimac valley they must have very swiftly learned the immense value of the tiniest drop of water in that arid environment, and from this realisation was born the complicated process of artificial irrigation which was to transform the dry sands into a little paradise for the envy and admiration of all future comers. But what tremendous efforts must have been made

PLATE III

(*Top*). Chinita's mask, made of woven cloth painted with red and blue stripes. Her hair-style, long and straight with a fringe at the front, is very similar to that worn by the Campas Indians who live today in the forests of the Amazon.

(*Left*). Our sorceress, pulling a very terrifying face. She has a nose made of a rounded piece of wood, hair of sisal grass dyed black, and skin made of some red material—a most impressive sight!

(*Right*). The Hunter's false head has a wooden nose stuck into it, and is made of cloth stuffed with rags; a red turban decorated with a few parrot's feathers holds the whole thing in place.

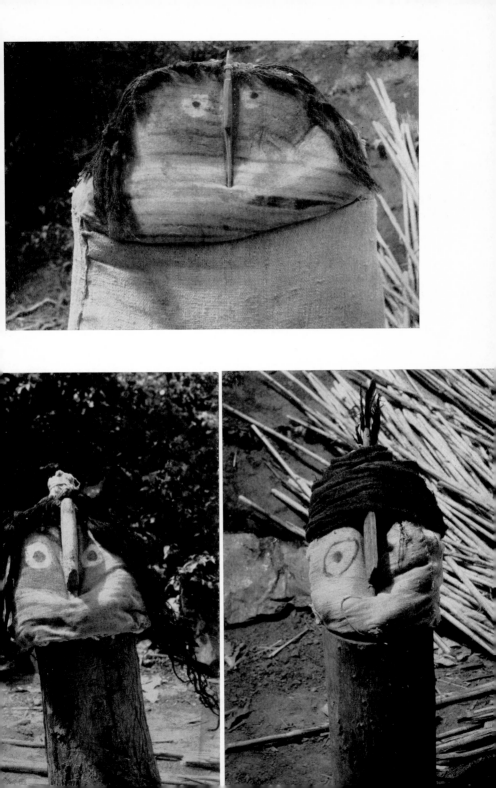

to coerce these parched sands to produce enough food to feed a whole tribe! What patient care must have led them to that love of the grudging earth and the generous sea whose fauna and flora were later to figure so largely in all their decorative art. All we could learn about the Wallas gave us a picture of a friendly, peace-loving, and hospitable people.

*   *   *

It was probably this idea of Walla hospitality that gave rise to the fable told by a peasant who cultivated the land bordering the Sugar Loaf *Waka*. He had heard it from a very old man who had lived on the Sugar Loaf *hacienda* at the time when its vast cotton fields covered all the land surrounding the pyramid. The old man had heard it from his great-grandfather.

It happened at the time when there were nothing but plantations all around the *waka*. One evening a young peasant was making his weary way towards the pyramid whose shadow stretched out along the Royal Way. At the corner of the *waka* stood a young Indian woman, watching him draw near, and he stopped and asked her the way. When she had told him, she asked him to wait a moment, and went into the *waka*; a moment later she emerged carrying three heads of Indian corn, which she handed to him, explaining that she gave these to all who travelled late along that road. He thanked her and asked her name, to which the Indian girl replied mysteriously:

PLATE IV

This extraordinary trio—the White Magician, the Sorceress and the Great Hunter—seem to be as fascinated by us as we were by them!

D

'I am the *waka*'. In due course the young man returned to his master's land, but when he took the corn out of his sack he found that it had turned into gold.

When he told his master this story, the great lord could not wait to try out his own luck, and asked the farmer to lead him straight away to the *waka*. They found the Indian woman standing at the same place and the landowner told her of his great desire to receive the same present as the other needy passers-by. The woman smiled, and signed to him to follow her. Hardly had they stepped inside when a great fragment of masonry fell on top of them and no one has been able to find the entrance to the *waka* since!

'You see,' added Castillo as he told us this story, 'the spirit of the *waka* wanted to punish the landowner's greed.'

For over four hundred years countless workmen have dug, sounded, and probed the mass of fallen debris which is still visible on the Royal Way. Frequently at night Castillo cannot sleep for thinking that there must be some way of finding the mysterious underground passage which, according to the gardener, must link the Sugar Loaf *Waka* to the *Waka* Juliana three-quarters of a mile away, and even to the pyramids of Maranga, further away still.

V

THE EVERYDAY LIFE OF THE WALLAS

Every one of the mummies of Peru is in itself a little museum of the past. More than one contemporary archaeologist has commented on the extraordinarily high value which the mummified figure bears as compared to the probable unimportance of the real person during his lifetime. Indeed their historical value is incalculable. Whatever these mysterious people (so carefully preserved in the tombs of Walla-Marka) were like in their own lifetimes, they certainly aroused our enthusiasm, and it is not really surprising that our hands should have trembled as they touched these strange great 'dolls', knowing that they held inside them the body of a man or woman, many centuries old.

One of our main subjects of discussion was whether the outward appearance of the mummy bore any resemblance at all to the real person who had been enclosed within it. The great false heads were of wood or fabric, the eyes were either paint or shells, and the hair was generally of sisal grass died black.

This discussion grew particularly heated with regard to the mummy whom we had christened Puccla, on account of his proud and commanding appearance. We used to chat about him quite naturally as one would discuss a living acquaintance. Imagine our consternation, therefore, when someone suggested that as we knew so little of the contents of the mummies it was perfectly possible that a figure bearing a masculine head might in fact contain the body of a woman! The fact that our beautiful Chinita might equally well be a handsome youth was of little consolation; but both Puccla and Chinita were rather perfect specimens, so we reluctantly resigned the temptation to open their wrappings, and agreed (albeit rather unwillingly) to wait until we had turned up a less immaculate specimen to help us to clear up this question.

For the time being we limited ourselves to placing Puccla and his train in their cultural epoch. This was another exciting adventure, for their dates—calculated by the most minute and careful examination and comparison—would either promote or weaken our theory that the Wallas were a tribe who had fled from Cuzco on the arrival of the Incas. Until then this theory had been supported only by the place-names cited by historians, and had no backing of material proof to substantiate it.

Not unnaturally, therefore, we were eager to have the verdict of the experts on the dating of our finds. It was considered that the mummies and ceramic utensils appeared to be of the Tiahuanaco type, and that Walla-Marka was the centre of a culture of transition containing elements of the last stage of the Maranga style together with the first influence of the Tiahuanaco.

This was exciting news indeed, but we still wanted to know more about the individual mummies which we had turned up. The objects buried with the first mummy might be ascribed to the Chancay style, which would make it later than the other mummies; the presence of ceramics of a kind ascribed only to Lima itself suggested a northern influence (the Chima), which was even more noticeable in the designs on the pottery, and a painted tunic.

Next it was our little Chinita's turn to be examined—her belongings were also Chancay; then the White Magician who was a little older, belonging to an epoch of transition from Tiahuanaco to Chancay; and finally, in chronological order—more and more remote in time although they all belonged to the same Tiahuanaco coastal culture—were our High Priestess with her long flowing hair, the Plumed Hunter, Puccla, and the Sorceress.

We were rather amused by the difficulty which the experts found

A TOMB IN THE SUGAR LOAF *Waka*

The tomb is 6 ft. 6 ins. high. It contained two *fardos*, a number of gourds, various earthenware pots and *wakos*. The left-hand *fardo* is the one which contained our 'High Priestess', with the immensely long hair. Fish bones and sea shells were found in the pots.

in identifying the mummies by the names we had given them, and which had replaced the usual numbers by which they had been listed in the field book. We found the names much more vivid; they seemed to make the mummies live again for a moment, and we hoped they would forgive us our audacity.

As the age of the mummies was so vital to our theories, it can be imagined with what anxiety we compared Bennet's chronology with our own: if only we could place the three most recent mummies somewhere between the fourteenth and fifteenth centuries, then the four earlier ones might indeed be those of Wallas who had emigrated from Cuzco at the date most people ascribe to the Inca invasion of their territory—1150—for the Tiahuanaco culture in which they had been placed lasted from A.D. 1000 to 1300.

★   ★   ★

Feeling considerably cheered, we wandered on to the balcony of our apartment dreaming of the days when Puccla, Chinita, the White Magician, the Sorceress, and the Plumed Hunter lived here in their huts of bamboo and sand; as they had done, we contemplated the distant horizon lost in the Pacific night, lifting our eyes to those same stars which they had adored, and finally drifting into a dream in which we, also explorers of unknown deserts, should find ourselves surrounded by unknown strangers, and around us would arise— called up by our fancies—the life of the mummies of Peru.

With a languorous gesture the High Priestess reached out for her comb of fine thorns held together by strands of brightly coloured cotton, and drew it slowly through her incredibly long silky hair. The moonlight shimmered on the arc of the silver bracelet encircling her tiny wrist. Had she seen us looking at her? The White Magician was gazing at us with his owl-like stare. What did he think of us? Smiling and carefree, a young girl dressed in a long tunic, with two magnificent red-and-blue parrots perched on her shoulders, squatted down beside the wall of the pyramid, and opened a little sewing-basket; she took out two little balls of cotton thread, one white and one brown; selecting a sharp little thorn to use as a needle, she did one or two embroidery stitches on a belt, and then gave that up in favour of threading the cotton on to a *puschka*—a long thorn, hard and black, with a carved head to hold the thread in place.

Suddenly the silence was broken by the wails of the Sorceress running wildly through our midst, distracted because she had seen some threat of earthquake or whirlwind in the unusual cloud formations which filled the sky, interpreting them as a message of destruction from her gods.

This warning made the face of the strange little man sunk in a corner turn even greener than before, and he already looked so ill that we would never have dared enquire after his health.

Our little Chinita was worried too as she looked at the walls of her hut, as if wondering if they were about to fall in on top of her. But Puccla was able to restore her confidence.

Delighted with the situation (that is, if you looked at him from the right side, for from the left he looked rather dismayed), he undertook to demonstrate to us the skill with which these little huts had been built, so that although they looked as if they would be blown over by the first breath of wind they could in fact quite easily withstand the periodic earthquakes which were frequent in that area.

We were invited to be Puccla's guests on a tour of the Walla village which surrounded the *waka*. We made our way across the fields, greeting on our way the men and women who crossed our path, dressed in tunics which they pinned up while working in the soil with a sharp little spear of hard wood. Some were digging holes, others putting in the seeds, and others covering them over with earth after inserting an anchovy head in each hole as a sort of fertiliser. From time to time we caught a whiff of the ammonia rising from the guano, which had been spread over the fields like some magic balm since time immemorial.

The Indian corn plantations were particularly well cultivated, and gave an abundant harvest twice a year; the Walla farmers also planted tapioca from which the women were able to make a drink, as well as a kind of bread and a fruit pudding. Besides these were broad beans, peppers, sweet potatoes, peanuts, marrows, and all sorts of vegetables we now know nothing of, flourishing in these sandy yet well-irrigated fields.

All around we saw bushes bending beneath the weight of their gourds, which would be made into plates when empty, or bowls, pans, or ladles, depending on their size and shape and the skill of the individual artist in carving and decorating them. Our path was fringed with trees which gave shade and delighted the eyes—guavas, pecans, avocados, figs, cactuses, and many other unfamiliar plants, nearly all bearing fruit with which to allay our hunger or quench our thirst.

Like Puccla, the Magician, and the Hunter, everyone we saw was wearing either a coloured turban or a length of coarse net wound like a turban round his head. Women with very long hair did likewise, although some had kept their hair short and straight like the men, and a few wore hair-nets and looked as if they had come straight from the hairdresser!

We followed a path between two walls made of great bricks of dried earth mixed with straw. The track stretched as far as the eye could see, and we learned from Puccla that if at any time it was covered over by sand blown in from the desert the traveller could still find his way by means of high stakes planted along it at regular intervals.

The vegetation reached right to the edge of the barren hills, and the desert only became true desert when it was steep or distant enough to defeat both man and river. Then all was desolate: the lonely sands stretching far into the distance visited only by the scorching sun or dark mists, with here and there the deceptive mirage of a lagoon mirroring pallid sky. Sand dunes like scorched loaves of bread stood out in these vast tracts of land, spotted only occasionally by lichen, by the rare tuberose or by a trail of moss, powdered over with sand. On the horizon, the sea and mountains joined in their mighty duet.

Suddenly a grey veil was stretched across the sun: the famous Pacific mist made us shiver, and the voice of the Spanish poet Juan de Arona, silent now for four centuries, came out of it like some strange mysterious message:

> The air draws on its cloak,
> And above us floats
> An indecisive but tenacious mist
> Incapable of melting
> Except in tiny drops.

This is a very apt description of this notorious mist, distilled in these regions by sky and ocean throughout the centuries.

Our dream had now led us into the Walla *marka* or village, where we saw the same little cube-shaped huts common throughout the Rimac valley. Each with its own little plot of ground, these were allocated by the village headman to each family according to size and the number of dependants.

'In the coastal region,' intoned Puccla in the monotonous style of a guide, 'there are two kinds of houses: one sort is made of canes interwoven with mud-covered rushes, has a flat roof covered with branches, and is admirably suited to withstand the storms which periodically lash the coast. The other kind is built of *tapia* (moulded earth) or mud bricks. Both varieties are built so that they are just big enough to hold one small family, and these little groups of huts form small clan centres, which are named *llakta* in the Quechua tongue and *marka* in Aymara. There is no tendency to urbanisation.'

Some huts were built on a base of forked trunks and branches of the various tropical trees growing in that valley. The horizontal roofs were firmly attached to the walls by sisal cords, and the whole construction was covered with a thin layer of mud.

Besides these huts there were the palaces, whose walls were covered in a rough-casting made of pounded sea shells similar to those which we had found on the terraces of the pyramids (although these were quite often painted in yellow ochre or red), and here and there we found little groups of even more primitive huts, containing only a platform of mud bricks for sitting or lying on, and built of twigs and branches covered with the leaves of Indian corn. These lay mainly beside the river Rimac, along whose banks many a colony has formed, from its source high in the mountains right down to the sea. It sleeps most of the time on its bed of rounded pebbles, only to awake from time to time in a mighty rage, shaking its great length and carrying away in fury some town built imprudently on its banks.

Our reveries were interrupted by the sight of men, women, and children returning to the village bowed down by the weight of the fruits and roots which they had been collecting. They laid these out on the ground to dry in the sunshine. As they went into their houses, we noticed that even the children had to bend down to go in and out, so low were the entrances.

Suddenly we spotted the plumed turban of a hunter just in sight behind a tree, and wondered what animal he was stalking. Was it a pigeon or a partridge, a turkey or wild duck? We hoped it was not one of the horrifying birds of prey with long red necks which roamed the skies around—and which formed a most economical cleansing department.

Certainly he would be well armed to catch any of these birds, for the Walla hunter had a long spear made of the hard *chonta* wood, as well as a sort of club or cudgel made of the same wood, and a curious sort of bow with one end fixed in the ground, a canvas band round the middle, and a weight on the top to increase the driving power.

What had he seen? An arrow flew through the air and pinned a thin little sand-coloured fox to the ground—whose pelt would later adorn the head of a *pariana*—the sentinel whose duty it was to guard the crops. We could see a *pariana* in the distance, his staff adorned with red pompoms, and his own body as thin as the little fox's, on account of the strict abstinence to which he was committed during his two months in office.

The houses were open in front, but well guarded by an army of noisy dogs. We could see ceremonial pottery, and we even saw some being made in a potter's hut: round, wide-necked pitchers ornamented with a geometrical design, and some remarkably beautiful ones with a vivid design of two serpents, their heads raised to strike. Another potter had chosen a lively puppet for his motif, while a third had modelled a terra-cotta human head with the round ears of a cat, crowned with a fretted coronet.

The ingenuity of the potter, and the vividness of his art, were indeed most striking. His brush was made of human hair tied tightly on to a little stick, while the powder-paints and vegetable juices which made up his other materials were kept in bamboo tubes or tiny clay pots.

The Walla women were no less artistic than the men. We saw one sitting in her hut, making a necklace so magnificent that it would be envied today by any wealthy fashionable woman. What looked like pearls were in fact thousands of tiny discs of mother-of-pearl, and these were being strung, alternating with turquoises, on to an astonishingly fine thread made of human hair plaited with cotton! A tiny pair of silver tweezers hung from the centre of the necklace.

One of her companions was working on a piece of fabric, painting flowing lines to represent the waves of the sea and patterns of wooden masks, clay heads, birds, fish, and flowers, and a cat arching its back and curling its tail (which is a pictorial theme to be found in all the coastal cultures).

The women doing embroidery were even more artistic, and under their agile fingers mythical heroes, gods, demons, beasts, and plants took shape, multicoloured and fantastic. These were strange, anthropomorphic shapes—each crowned with the same moon-shaped diadem and encircled by a belt representing two serpents—wearing chinstraps and brandishing shields or bucklers as they advanced, either alone or encircled by a ballet of dancing fish and seaweed. We had seen seaweed like this filling the baskets of the fishermen on their way home, to be welcomed by the entire village population. They also carried shellfish of many kinds, crabs, lobsters, and fish, for the sea around the Peruvian coastline is the richest in the world and the beaches washed by mighty waves abound in mussels and scallops.

All the women took a hand in preparing the fish, some gutting it, some cutting the larger ones into pieces to salt and dry them in the sun, either on specially prepared terraces or on the flat roofs of the houses beside the seaweed, both of which were most jealously guarded as dehydrated foods for exchange with other tribes.

One or two women stayed in the huts, but far from being inactive they were engaged either in plaiting and knotting tall rafia crowns or spinning a web of lace so fine that the most ingenious spider would have been jealous of it. We might have gone on admiring these works of art much longer had not Puccla pointed out that a sand storm had arisen which threatened to make our journey to the next village most unpleasant if not impossible.

On the way back we met a warrior carrying the most vicious weapon of that time, the *porra*, a heavy pointed stone club, fixed on to a long stick. It must have been such a warrior who, because of some personal quarrel, had wounded the man we had seen in the village surrounded by the doctors and healers of the clan. Already someone had shaved his head and gathered up the fragments of broken bone, which they tied up in a piece of cloth ready to bury with him should he die, and when he had cleaned the wound the surgeon covered it with a cotton dressing protected by a piece of gourd, which in turn was held on by a net pulled over the victim's head.

The whole village was in an uproar of indignation, and in spite of the fact that his victim was not even definitely dead, the assailant had already received his punishment and preparations were being made for his burial. We could see that he must have been an important person by the splendour with which he was being prepared for his last journey.

The first step was to arrange the body in the customary position for burial, the knees drawn up to the chin and pieces of cotton placed in the nose and mouth, while a silver chinstrap was fixed by a knotted cord to the blue turban, which gave him the appearance of a Bedouin. He was wrapped round and round in layer after layer of cloth which the women had woven on their simple looms. Then came the most splendid garment of all—a sort of *poncho* or toga sewn all over with brilliant parrot feathers. How many birds must have been sacrificed to make this festive garment! But then nothing is too beautiful for the other world, which opens its doors on to the terrace of a *waka*, one side of which is reserved for the men, the other for women.

A carved wooden head with reddened cheeks was fixed on top of the mummified figure, after which it was lowered into a sort of well, the sides of which had been strengthened with branches. This simple tomb was then filled up with sand, and a cover of interwoven reeds placed on top, leaving no sign of the presence of the mummy except for a single bamboo which stuck out into the upper world as a signal from the dead man to any relative coming to join him.

The ceremonial rites accompanying burial were striking in their majesty, and were aptly described by P. las Casas in the sixteenth century: 'Along the coast the burials of important personnages took place in public, and the burial mounds were surrounded by choirs of women singing songs in praise of the deeds and virtues of the dead man.'

Would we be asked to take part in the ritual banquet? Yes, for already the High Priestess, her hair trailing like a comet behind her, was leading us towards a magnificent table laden with pottery dishes and gourds decorated with fretwork. On one of these dishes, which was filled with corn, was depicted a lifelike demon cat, fur ruffled and whiskers bristling, crawling along on little velvet feet. One gourd plate was covered with a design of little irridescent fish, rather like smelt, another was covered with a pale and dark brown check, while a third (which held a roasted guinea-pig) was decorated with a circle of pelicans flying round the perimeters.

When we had finished eating we suddenly thought of having a look at the bottom of our bowls. Yes, they were signed—not with a name, but with the design of a heart enclosed between two scrolls. Was this the signature of the artist? The owner's mark? Or was it perhaps an indication of what the dish was intended to hold? Similar marks have been found on Chancay pottery and on Paracan materials. Could it be some mysterious alphabet? We could not be sure, but of one thing we were certain: the ingenuity and artistry of these faraway peoples was remarkably highly developed.

★   ★   ★

We still felt an integral part of our surroundings when we woke up the following morning, after our extraordinarily vivid dream, to see Puccla with his silent but so theatrically alive-looking court. No wonder they had made us feel at home with them: they were so like us, so human-looking; completely different from the Egyptian mummies, rigidly upright in their wooden coffins with their cloth cocoons so geometrically perfect that it is impossible to believe they had ever been alive, such is the calm unreality of their aspect.

On the contrary, the Peruvian mummies seem full of expression, and the mock faces seem to have been fashioned with varying expressions—surprise, horror, fear, and resignation, all are to be found carved into these primitive heads, giving them an uncanny air of reality. So much did these expressions influence our idea of the characters contained within that we could almost imagine them wandering around in their after-life, clad in their painted or embroidered coats, their feathered tunics, with exactly the personality which we had assumed from their mock faces.

Small wonder then that we listened intently outside the door of the work-hut, opening the door gingerly to allow a shaft of light to pierce the darkness and reveal our friends the High Priestess, Puccla, the Wizard, and all the others sitting propped up against the walls seeming to await our visit, and to answer our smiles of greeting with an understanding nod of the head.

VI

MUNAOS AND MALLKIS

The excavation of the pre-Columbian tombs in Peru is one of the most important chapters in the book of world archaeology, for when we caught our first glimpse of these thousands of mummies, hidden until then under the desert sands or interred in the *chullpa* (a round or quadrangular burial tower) of the mountain tribes, we were given vivid proof of a race which until then had been legendary.

How intrigued we were by the contents of these pyramids and tombs! Take for example the cloth or wooden masks which crowned the Walla mummies: why should they have these enormous round eyes staring out of their heads, so different from the almond shape on the 'portrait' *wakas* to be found in the burial mounds of the Mochica-Chimu or the Nazcas? Was it because they were made of shells? It would surely have been easy enough to carve these to shape, especially for a people whose artistic prowess was so clearly demonstrated on their pottery, their drinking gourds, and their fabrics. Of course, not many of the mummies with cloth or wooden heads were those of particularly rich or noble people. These were to be found—and there must be many thousands still uncovered—sleeping beneath their northern sands, their faces and hands protected by a mask of reddish-gold.

The tombs in which these wealthier mummies were laid were known, along the coast, by the names of *machais* or *zamays*, both words meaning 'place of rest'. In these were buried those considered as the fathers of the clan, whose bones or mummified bodies would be called in that coastal region *munaos*, while in the mountain districts they were known as *mallkis*; the name *munao* appears to be derived from *munay*, meaning 'to love, to want, to cherish', while *mallki* means 'the mixture of the seed with the earth'. This explanation underlined what we already knew of these peoples' love and veneration for their ancestors, an emotion which they called *cayaspa*, and which they inherited with all their other traditions, superstitions, rites, and religious beliefs.

How did they preserve their mummies? What was this process which could guard them from the rigours of centuries, and which was still being practised at the time of the Spanish invasion? It seems that this is a secret which the Indians were determined never to reveal, and we are reduced to the same guess-work as the chroniclers at the time of the Spanish conquest, alike in our inability to solve the mystery and our admiration for the people whose secret it has remained.

PLATE V

These frightening sculptured wooden masks display great round eyes made out of shells staring out of reddened faces with blue-painted mouths. Three of them have holes punched in the top of their foreheads to hold their false hair in place; the other has a piece sticking out on top of his head to hold a turban.

These 'crowns' made of vegetable fibre are oval or square-shaped, and very closely resemble the crowns worn by the Mashiguengas, a semi-civilised Indian tribe from the Urubamba.

One of the chroniclers, Gomara, believed that the bodies of the mummies were embalmed by anointing with resinous substances and by pouring purifying liquids obtained from tropical trees down the throat; a modern botanist cites a shrub with orangy-red flowers known as the *aya-aya*, which he believes to have been one of the ingredients used by the Incas for the preservation of their mummies.

Another theory is that the mummies were impregnated with some bituminous substance, while the eyes were delicately dusted with gold. (Tablets of gold or silver were also used to cover the nose and mouth and sometimes even the hands and chest, while the face was reddened with a vermilion dye.)

There is also Blas Valera's story of the burials of kings and nobles, whose tombs were 'like very dwelling-houses, with all the habita-

PLATE VI

A loom with the half-finished work still intact, showing the famous 'ladder' motif—a symbol of the union of the earth and sun—which occurs constantly in the art of all the ancient civilisations of South and Central America.

The basket-work of the pre-Columbian civil-isations along the Pacific coast of Peru is highly skilled, both artistically and technically. The tall basket is very practical for carrying the spin-ning bobbins, while the rectangular sewing-basket holds countless little balls of white or coloured cotton, together with needles made of thorn. In the foreground there is an empty half-gourd containing the heads of Indian corn ex-cavated from the *wakas*.

E

tions of a normal house, living rooms, bedrooms, kitchen, *patio*, and corridors . . .', and, he adds, 'once the king was dead they took out his intestines and embalmed the body with a balm brought from Tolú, and other spices; and in this way the body would last for four or five hundred years.'

Some scholars describe alternative methods such as smoking the body like a ham or filling it with hot cinders, and there are some who believe that the holes which are so frequently found drilled in the skulls of the mummies were made in order to clean out the skull and possibly to pour in aromatic oils which would prevent the brain from rotting.

There is one point, however, on which many writers are in agreement, and that is that the Incas did not use preservatives like the Egyptians; once they had removed the corpses' intestines it is generally supposed that they left the rest to the divine power of the Sun-father, helped by the nocturnal frosts and the dry mountain air; while in the coastal regions it is almost certain that the dry heat and chemical content of the sand would preserve the bodies without any necessity for embalming.

★   ★   ★

It was the sixty-ninth ruler of the first dynasty, Aranial Cassi, who invented the mysterious process or processes used in mummifying the bodies of kings, and his name in Quechua means 'he who sets the mummies in order'. It was he who started the cruel custom of sacrificing the king's favourite women with him. When he embalmed his father's corpse, we are told that he first took out the liver and the heart before treating them with 'certain aromatic confections'.

Whatever these processes of conservation may have been, it is almost certain that the funeral rites had very definite religious significance. We have no proof that the dead were worshipped—it is more likely that the living were trying to make their life in the other world longer and more pleasant, and of protecting them from bad spirits. Certainly the Jesuit Blas Valera disagreed emphatically with the opinion that the Peruvians adored their dead as if they were possessed of some divine virtue.

'On the contrary,' says Blas Valera, 'they prayed to the great Illa Tecce to look after the dead man, not to let his body be spoilt and lost in the earth, not to allow his soul to wander, but to gather it in and keep it in some region of happiness.' As for the offerings or sacrifices made to the dead man, these were put in the care of the supreme divinity to give to the dead for their use in the after-life. These burial offerings were in fact almost certainly destined for the bodily necessities of the mummies, who were deemed to lead a similar life in the other world to the one they had led in this. Occasionally, however, burial offerings may have been intended as magic charms to protect them from the demons who were believed to be responsible for the decomposition of the body.

In one of these alternative purposes must lie the explanation of the number of leaves, seeds, nuts, branches, and roots to be found included in the mummies' funeral packages—all of which are still used by the Indians of today, who are fully conscious of the useful properties of each one of them.

For instance, *coca* leaves are considered to be energy-producing, and are chewed continuously by the Andean Indian to make him forget his hunger and give him stoical endurance. We have seen *coca* leaves placed in bags of seed potatoes in the belief that they will encourage a better crop.

There is a legend about the *coca* plant. In the days of Purun Pacha, when the earth was peopled by wild beasts and wicked spirits and covered with a hostile jungle, a goddess descended to earth carrying a child in her arms. As she was very tired she sat down beneath a *coca* tree and spread the child's clothes along its branches. Now up till that time the *coca* tree had been evil and poisonous, but from the moment the goddess asked it for shelter it became a good tree whose leaves gave vigour and strength to all who ate them, and whose sap was able to combat hunger and exhaustion. The leaves are also said to possess a protective power which keeps away demons of the air, pain, and death.

Another legend explains the presence in the tombs of the *pacao* flower, and we learnt that the flowers of the gentian and the leaves of the *secsec* were both considered efficacious against sorcery and domestic troubles, which was why we were able to buy them on the Friday of Holy Week, woven into a T-shape and sold under the name of *nihua-Cruz*. There was also the Inca flower, the *kantuta*, which has been grown throughout the centuries and has always been considered to have magic powers, so that even today the Indians will put it in their tombs believing it to have the power of assuaging thirst in the other world. The roots of the *chucam* too are still chewed by the Indians when they set off on one of their interminable wanderings over the mountains, as well as the red seeds of the *huayrure*, which are tipped with black and have such astonishing efficacy against melancholia that no Indian woman is ever without one or two grains in her purse, while the mummies wear them dangling round their necks in a long necklace. The berries of the astringent *pichurim*, tobacco leaves, the rosaries made of the nuts of a certain tree—all these and many others are associated with magic qualities.

Whatever part we believe these things to have played—whether as food for the dead man's stomach or protection for his spirit—it is almost certain that the pre-Incas and Incas both believed in re-incarnation, even if in animal form, and that because of this the disintegration of the physical body was what they most feared. This explains the action of the Inca Atahualpa, who when condemned by the Spaniards to be burned alive chose instead to be baptised and then strangled, so that his body might not disappear in smoke. Archaeology can provide us with countless examples of this desire to safeguard the body, as for example the many skeletons found with the spinal vertebrae carefully threaded on to a bamboo, to prevent them from falling apart.

VII

THE FUNERAL RITES OF THE INCAS

I f in the following chapter we compare the life of the Inca *mallkis* with that of the pre-Inca mummies, it is because not only is the history of the Cuzco Incas and the Lima Wallas linked from the start, but that the proof of their connection was to be found in the very place we were working—Lima itself. Everything seems to point to the fact that the important parts of the Inca funeral rites corresponded closely to those of the pre-Inca Wallas, and even if we have no actual written testimony of these we do have plenty of information in the chronicles of the Spanish conquest, which give us details not only of the Inca customs but also of those of the Yungas, who lived in Lima at the time.

How solemn and august were the obsequies of an Inca ruler: sensational processions accompanied by heart-rending lamentations and funeral chanting, with dancing figures weaving around the high gold-crowned litter, upon which the mummy was going on his last journey.

Several years after the conquest a chronicler saw the funeral of the Inca Titu Cusi being celebrated at Vilacamba, on the outskirts of Cuzco. This ceremony, he tells us, was called *purucalla* (meaning 'funeral honours'), and consisted of a great procession of eminent men, all in heavy mourning, each of whom carried some possession of the dead king—his clothes, his hat, his turban, shoes, armour, jewels, royal insignia, and standard—all of which were borne along to the accompaniment of the rolling of drums and the piercing sobs and cries of the women.

The moment he was safely installed in his last resting place (the doors and windows of which were closed after they had placed all his treasures, pottery, and clothes in the ante-chamber and made sure that he had plenty of bread and wine), a crier announced that any of the dead man's servants, friends, or allies who would like to go and serve him in the other life could now do so of their own free will; and if they chose to do so they would be rewarded by the great Illa Tecce Viracocha, creator of sun, moon, and stars, and of all the other gods; moreover, the particular god of the dead man's family would look upon them favourably in the other life and give them an abundance of all good things; the children and heirs of those who decided to serve the dead man would be allotted special grants of land and other worldly possessions. Anyone who did not wish to accompany the dead man should at all events help him by making the necessary offerings.

The Jesuit Blas Valera tells us that those who obeyed this summons and offered themselves as servants in the after-life could either take their own lives or find someone else to kill them; they were given the choice of hanging, knifing, being thrown to wild beasts or over a precipice, taking poison, and other attractive alternatives. They would then be embalmed and placed in the ante-chamber if they were men, or with the material possessions if they were women.

Blas Valera goes on to say that these candidates for sacrifice could still escape death by offering numerous presents in their place, having explained publicly and before magistrates the reason for their change of heart. These presents usually consisted of clothing or cattle, sacrificed with great solemnity; in this way a thousand llamas were sacrificed on the death of the great Inca, Huayna Kapak. Blas Valera adds dryly that this exchange of lives against presents was such common practice among the ancient Peruvians that hardly anyone died unaccompanied by a great many cattle, and whenever the sacrifice was over there was great celebration and feasting by those who had thus satisfied the dead man while escaping with their lives.

Sarmiento de Gamboa explains that the *purucalla* consisted also of spectacular mimes which took place in public, often in front of the temple of the sun, and which celebrated the great achievements and triumphs of the dead. Bards and poets would sing the dead man's praises in odes and ballads. These epic litanies all began with a phrase similar to our 'once upon a time', guaranteed to capture the interest of the audience the moment it has been spoken. They were then relayed by word of mouth throughout the whole empire of Tahuantinsuyo on great feast days or on the eve of battles.

★　　★　　★

It is well known that on the greatest agricultural feast day of the Inca year (the famous Inti Raymi) all the royal mummies were on show in the vast Aucaypata square in Cuzco—all, that is, since the reign of Manko Kapak. It was the custom for the soothsayers and the servants who had special charge of each mummy to appear before the reigning monarch and recount their master's deeds, those of Manko Kapak being the first to appear, and the others following in chronological order. Each mummy was carried on a throne under a parasol of multicoloured feathers, and in the evening all joined in a solemn procession which, to the sound of solemn music, wound its way to the fabulous Coricancha, the 'Place of Gold', temple of the sun.

The same ceremonies were carried out on the *Citua*, the famous feast of purification, during the course of which the dancers, dressed in long red tunics and playing Indian flutes, danced the *alaua Citua taqui* in front of the mummies. According to Dr. J. B. Lastres, this was a prophylactic measure.

According to the chroniclers, it was in the hall reserved in honour of the sun that they placed the embalmed Incas, while the *coyas* (or legitimate wives) were to be found lined up in two rows on silver-backed benches. Seated in their triangular niches adorned with idols, their faces turned towards the sacred town (all except the mummy of Huayna Kapak, the only one who dared look directly at the marvellous carved golden disc, representing the Sun God) several of the mummies were crowned by a mask—generally that of a fox.

The mummies were taken out into the sunshine several times each year, in order to prevent their clothes rotting. The body of Huayna Kapak was quite often to be seen being carried into the square, accompanied by music and dancing, with servants standing by him, night and day, to chase away the flies.

Indeed, each Inca *mallki* was served in death as in life with the same devoted and elegant attention. Food and drink were brought to him at meal-times, his clothes were looked after, his lands cared for, and his llamas encouraged to multiply in order to satisfy his ultra-terrestrial needs. His clowns went on with their drollery, and his tailor, his perfumers, his dancers, musicians, and pages continued to devote their time to him.

Pedro Pizarro, the young cousin and page of the famous *conquistador*, explains how each Inca was buried together with all his important possessions. A similar importance was attached to the things the dead man had left behind in his house—for instance the rush mat on which he had been accustomed to rest. Thus we have the famous story of the Inca Atahualpa, who remained quite unmoved by the sight of the Spaniards carrying off his treasures but flew into a storm of rage when they laid their hands on a mat in the chamber where his father, Huayna Kapak, used to sleep.

Pedro Pizarro also tells us that if the Inca was buried with his wives, one carried his jewels, another his drinking cups, and the others his plates of wood and silver; moreover, one cook and one washerwoman were chosen to help him in the after-life.

National mourning in honour of these monarchs lasted at least six months, and the sacrifices and offerings continued during this time, while for the first month the entire populace observed a restricted diet which permitted them neither salt nor pepper.

That the mummies were most realistic even in death is corroborated by the extraordinary tale of a young Inca captain, who was granted permission by the Spaniards to marry a young Indian girl on condition that he asked her parents for her hand in front of a Spanish witness. Imagine the latter's amazement when, on going forward to congratulate the young bride sitting clad in all her wedding finery between her chattering parents, he found that her look of chilly remoteness was all too explicable—she was, in fact, a mummy.

The custom of displaying the mummies in processions on certain important days was not a special Inca prerogative and Cieza de Leon (speaking of the customs which were current in the district around Lima) writes:

> When the dead man had been an important lord they used to take out his mummified body once a year and carry it in state around his lands, where the people acclaimed him as if he had still been alive. When this had been done they reburied the mummy with much pomp, singing his praises and watering the grave with the blood of women, children, and llamas who were sacrificed then rather than on the day of his actual death. All this ceremony was accompanied by funereal chanting—all the remaining great men of the village came together to lament, and the women shaved off all their hair as a demonstration of grief.

This chronicler also informs us that the great men of the Yunga tribe had many wives, and each one tried to outdo the other in the number and beauty of his women. Which ones were chosen to go with him into the next world? The choice was made between the most beautiful of the women, and was not necessarily the first or the legitimate favourite, as one of the others might recently have supplanted her.

Huaman Poma tells us that in Inca times there was a custom, still practised by the Indians of that region, by which the widow, parents, brothers, and sisters of the deceased meet together five days after his death to see whether they would soon have to join the dead man in the grave. This was a curious custom: every village had a little cave with two openings; a stream was directed through this cave, and if it was in any way held up in its passage, it was thought to be a bad sign and the relatives would surely die very soon. In some places the villagers built a little runlet down a slope; the widow poured water in at the top end, and if it ran out rapidly this was a good sign and she was not going to die. As a sign that this curious ceremony had been carried out the widow took off her belt, her turban, or her sandals.

Occasionally these tests were carried out when the widow washed her dead husband's clothes. If the test was successful she stretched black and white yarn across from the river for all to see, and everyone sang and made merry, drinking and dancing all night long.

Widows did not return to their own families, but remained in their husband's clan and became the property of his eldest brother. If the husband had no brother, they were allowed to remarry after a year of strict mourning.

Along the Lima coast it was the custom for the whole of the dead man's family to reunite ten days after his death and to plunge his nearest relative three times into the river where the dead man's clothing was being washed. This ceremony was followed by a ritual feast in which the first mouthful tasted had to be spat out. When the feast was over, all the *chicha* which was left was sprinkled over the ground so that the soul of the dead man could quench his thirst and then everyone went joyfully home with a clear conscience feeling that the deceased had been safely sped on his way to the after-life.

If for some reason or other this ritual bath and banquet were considered inadequate, one of the widows would be buried alive beside the mummified corpse to console him after death. When this happened the woman was first drugged with *coca* powder.

The widespread belief in the mummies' continuing bodily needs meant that there were frequent banquets held by their tombs, at which the ground was generously sprinkled with *chicha* and llama fat was burnt. We ourselves had seen such banquets at Recuay in the Cordillera Blanca, where the Indians, picnicking on tombs surrounded by high cacti and aloes, were weeping and dancing to the sound of wavering flutes and a violin scratched and scraped by a native priest.

The Indians of Huarochiri and Yauyos (who lived in the mountains above Lima) would bring out their mummies once a year to clothe them anew, and for three days and nights they were on view on the mountain tops, while around them there was great feasting and revelry. This was one of the most important ceremonies of the pagan year, when the mummies' food and drink supplies were renewed, so that they should suffer neither hunger nor thirst.

VIII

LUGGAGE FOR THE PRE-INCA AFTER-LIFE

These mummies, as we have seen, were buried with the greatest wealth of materials, jewels, and other objects, and it is time to take a closer look at this funeral 'luggage' which as in most of the advanced ancient civilisations accompanied the dead man into his after-life.

We had already seen in the Canta mountains near Lima the most extraordinary *mallkis* tied up in sacks made of llama skins, with only their ghostly heads poking out at the top. Underneath these leather bindings (which made the mummy look just like a barrel) was a thick layer of *coca* leaves and wads of raw cotton. This was followed by long strips of cloth wound repeatedly round him, and finally there were the actual garments, sometimes worn, sometimes just laid on top of the body, which were really beautiful and looked not unlike fine tapestries. The false head wore a *llauto* or turban in vicuna, which imitated real hair, and was either left straight or plaited in numerous little pigtails, as worn today by the Colla Indians on the high plains surrounding Lake Titicaca or the Quechuas of the Urubamba sacred valley. Sometimes they were also adorned with multicoloured plumes. One of these *mallkis* was found among the other mummies in the Walla-Marka, but in an advanced state of decay.

Mummies are much more numerous in the burial chambers under the sand of the magnificent Ancon bay, a few miles north of Lima, where it is thought that more than thirty thousand mummies lie buried. These are also sometimes sewn or bound in the hides of foxes, deer, jaguars, or even seals, some apparently related to the northern Chimus; if true, this would be a remarkable instance of cultural cross-breeding. The lobes of their ears are weighed down and stretched by enormous rings of wood or carved bone, inlaid with tiny pieces of red or white shell, or by discs of gold or sometimes even by simple rolled palm leaves, and decked out with amulets and charms. We have even seen the mummies being led into the other world by a short-haired spotted dog, also mummified and attached to his master by a leash of human hair.

On one occasion when we unearthed the head of a young Apollo, we were surprised to see that he had short hair, until we noticed the reason for this unusual feature; fleas—now mummified—had abounded there! The head was protected by a finely woven basket, and a similar plaited shield was placed on his chest. He was dressed in a fringed tunic with a border of brown hieroglyphics on a pinkish background, and his mask was a poignant one with two painted tears falling from the round eyes.

Some mummies had hands tattooed in yellow or red, while strange little bamboo crosses bound with coloured thread were laid across their bodies. Others were covered with their ceremonial coat of arms, painted on cloth tightly stretched between bamboo struts, on which strange creatures were painted wearing half-moon helmets, surrounded by scrolls and little circles which might have been eggs (symbols of life in embryo), drops of water, or bubbles of air.

The most important people sometimes carried a ceremonial staff, banded with brightly coloured thread which was woven into geometrical designs, with a cord at one end from which hung a sort of tassel made of feathers or oddments of cloth, and occasionally hung with jewels.

We had also seen mummies wearing the *chullo*, a sort of bonnet with earflaps and a peak worn by the Indians of the Andes, and one wore a cowl of woven sisal grass, the same material as was used for their *espadrille*-type shoes. This one was also supplied with a store of rounded stones of the type used in their slings, a polishing instrument made of bone, a corn grater, and a large-eyed copper needle.

A TOMB IN THE SUGAR LOAF *Waka*

This tomb contained five *fardos*, measuring from 2 ft. 10 ins. to 3 ft. 10 ins. in height and from 1 ft. 5 ins. to 2 ft. in width.

One object which turned up repeatedly in the tombs was the *quena*, a kind of Indian flute. Owing to its shape, this was considered as a symbol of masculinity, and it is therefore possible that it did not denote musical ability in the mummy whom it accompanied, but was simply there as a charm to ensure strength and fertility in his future life.

The music of the *quena* was not always intended for human ears, but was often played to the animals, mountains, and waters, as well as to the spirits of the great mountain range itself, for music in these regions has always been greatly inspired by the surrounding countryside.

Nearly all the *quenas* found with the mummies were made out of reeds or the bones of llamas or deer; very few of those made of condor bone remained, although we knew that they existed; presumably this bone, being more fragile than the other materials, was less able to resist the destructive action of the centuries.

Rather to our surprise, the flutes found in the Walla-Marka, which were made of llama bone, all lacked the notched mouthpiece which we had, until then, considered as an essential part of the instrument. This unusual feature tempted some members of our party to take them back to their quarters and try them out for themselves, and you can imagine our surprise when we were greeted by them one evening with what sounded like a fully fledged native concert! It certainly proved that these ancient flutes were as good as any of today, and conversely that our modern musicians were just as skilled as those depicted on the pottery of the Chancay or Pachacamac periods. These scenes show us pictures of the Yunga tribes at work in the cultivation of the land with their flutes slung across their backs, and several of the *quenas* found actually had the ring by which they were slung round the neck, just like an *ocarina* flute. These also were found among the possessions in the graves, and were made out of baked clay, in the shape of birds. Was this shape indicative, perhaps, of their functions? They may have been used for scaring birds out of the corn? Or perhaps their note was a warning signal?

Alternatively, they may have been used as we had seen them used among the Chunco Indians, as a way of directing the dancers.

We found another kind of flute—the *sicu*—buried with the mummies. This is a kind of pipes of Pan, and is still played in Peru today; its strange melody can be heard weaving its notes around the shores of Lake Titicaca, leaving its hearers amazed at the virtuosity of its player—the *sicuri*—whose rapid notes (known as male or female, according to their tone) fill the air in a sort of musical conversation.

There were also *sicus* made of pottery, but these all seemed to have been broken intentionally before being laid in the tombs. We wondered whether this might perhaps have some connection with an ancient Mexican custom based on the legend of the young

PLATE VII

A little bag in very fine cotton lace; a carved and painted wooden box; a tapestry band of material in many colours dating from the Tiahuanaco epoch: all evince the extraordinary artistic skill of the first inhabitants of San Isidro—now a residential quarter in modern Lima. These objects, which are all nearly a thousand years old, are on display in the museum at the foot of the pyramid.

Necklaces made of pearl-like shells, one of which is adorned by a tiny pair of bird-shaped silver tweezers. The thick bracelets and the ceremonial vase are made of beaten and engraved silver. Similar silver vases were thrown into the sacred lakes when children were sacrificed to the gods Wallallo and Pariakaka.

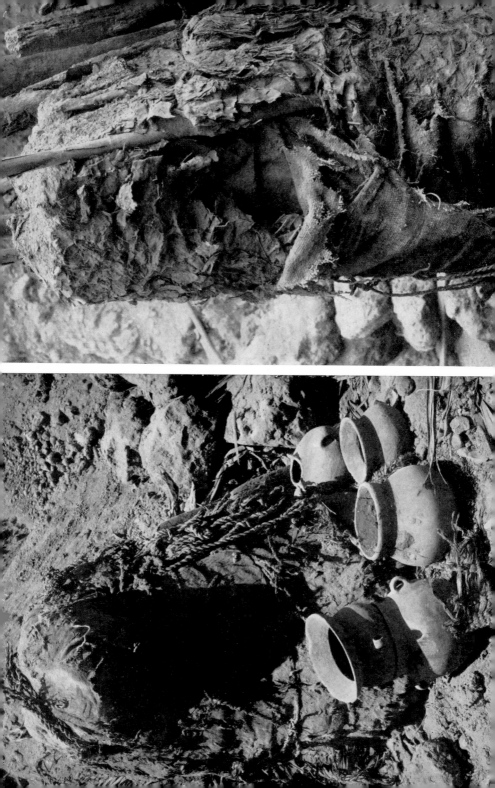

Aztec flautist who, when condemned to die on the top of a pyramid, ascended the steps of his pyramid playing a different tune on each step, and breaking the flute with which it had been played as he moved to the next step.

The women lay beside their men, carrying their little spindles of half-wound wool and looking for all the world just like the Indian women we had met so often, picking their way across the heights of the frozen Andes behind their great herds of disdainful-looking llamas. Round their waists they wore a broad tapestry belt woven with pastoral scenes in many colours, just like the ones we can buy today in the market; this was used to hold their looms in place. These looms posed yet another problem, for one has never yet been found which would have been big enough to take the winding-cloths which were frequently almost five feet wide.

On their backs they carried the *lliclla* (a large square of woven material) which they folded into a triangle and fastened securely at the front with a *tupu* (a large carved silver pin, looking rather like a soup spoon).

Many of the mummies had little boxes—some empty, some containing necklaces made of tiny pearl-like shells, of metal, of gold, of

PLATE VIII

The figure of a mummy appeared wrapped in a coarsely-woven net. Near by were some utilitarian pottery containers holding black beans, peanuts, and a little bag of woven reeds. This mummy was not nearly so well preserved as some of the others excavated in the Sugar Loaf *Waka.*

F

pottery, and of wood, bracelets and long strings of beads so artistic in their form and colouring that they would grace the window of the most elegant jeweller of today.

Let us listen to the simple and precise words of Huaman Poma as he describes the funeral customs of the Yungas:

> the Indians of the coast wail and cry, repeating 'Nanu, Nanu, Nanu' (what sadness, what grief, what pain!), they drink themselves into a stupour, then they fast.

He then continues—illustrating his words with sketches which would make any modern illustrator envious—that before burying their people they removed the intestines and took the skin from the flesh, which was then wrapped in a cotton cloth and sewn in securely, or held well in place with cords called *tocllas*, and finally painted. The finished result was placed in a sitting position in a room beside the father, the mother, or others belonging to the same *ayllu* or clan. We nearly always found four or five figures sitting next to each other in the same funeral chamber, and sometimes even wrapped in the same bundle.

It was during the work of restoration on the Puruchucu Palace that an extremely rare and beautiful set of *kipus* was found. *Kipus* were the knotted and multicoloured cords used by the Incas in their mysterious system of keeping notes and accounts.

The set was found in a large pottery jar, about five centuries old, and consisted of two new-looking cords without any knots at all, about a dozen knotted all the way down, and another dozen knotted only half-way. These made up the complete 'account book' of the great lord of Puruchucu, whose mummy was found lying in great splendour in a neighbouring room—a sort of funeral chamber built only a few yards from the palace.

The Puruchucu *kipus* are of greater interest than most others in private collections and museums, simply because we know very definitely to whom they belonged. Besides, although they resembled other *kipus* in being made up of various coloured cords of different thicknesses, each of which was knotted in many different ways, these ones also had many extras such as a whole series of cords made up into bundles, as well as pieces of finer cord, and tassels in brown, fawn, yellow, red, and grey, all of which must have made it possible for the *kipukamayoc* in this great agricultural centre to keep detailed records of crops and tributes.

★ ★ ★

The most touching feature of the whole excavation was the finding of the little mummified bodies of children, each carrying its tiny wooden doll, a favourite bird, or some tiny pottery dishes.

One of the most puzzling of our discoveries was a plaything found with the body of a baby buried under the Ica sands to the south of Lima. It looked just like a small-scale model of one of the balsa rafts of which the *Kon Tiki* and the *Tahiti Nui* were modern copies. At first no one had any doubt that this was a perfect little replica of one of the craft of two millennia ago, with its keel about five feet long, with the cabin—eighteen inches long and seven high—made of small sticks of bamboo lashed together, placed towards the prow. But when news of this fascinating and hitherto unparalleled discovery reached the rest of the world, other theories were thought up and doubts began to creep in. Was it really a balsa raft? Might it not have been a bird snare? Or even the baby's cradle? Could it be the very instrument they used for piercing the skull, causing the mysterious gashes we had found in the skulls of our skeletons? Nobody knew, and we were forced to leave this particular mystery unsolved.

At about the same time there was another most interesting find, by Yoshitaro Amano, who discovered a little vase of artificial flowers attached to the side of a tomb in the Chancay valley. They were very beautifully made, of tiny pieces of brightly coloured material bound together with cotton thread.

There is still a tremendous amount to be discovered about these ancient Peruvian civilisations, much of whose lore has come to us second hand from ancient chronicles and manuscripts.

It must constantly be borne in mind that archaeology is still a relatively new science in Peru. Indeed there are many strange stories arising from the 'mystery' which surrounded the new science, one of the most amusing of which relates how a young student was denounced to the police by an over-zealous little boy, whose suspicions had been aroused by the number of strangely shaped and sometimes evil-smelling packages carried into Tello's house; he peered through the keyhole and saw Tello himself gloating over his 'victims', who were of course nothing more or less than his greatly prized collection of mummies!

The total ignorance of the whole uneducated population of Peru is of course well known to any foreign tourist who has set foot outside Lima, only to find himself besieged by crowds of peasants ostensibly working for some landowner in the vicinity but in reality gaining their living by selling the relics which they remove almost daily from the tombs. Although the tourist is unlikely at first to know anything of the value of what he is being offered, he can hardly help being attracted by the beauty and strangeness of the pottery, necklaces, bracelets, baskets, and masks offered him by these half-naked ragged children. If tempted to follow them back to their little village of straw huts built along the edge of one of the great main roads leading out of Peru, he will then probably be amazed to see the same physiognomy, the same bronzed skin, hooked nose, and narrowed eye, that he has already noticed on the masks and pottery figures. The archaeological models of huts, with little figures busy with their task of grinding corn between two stones, can also be found translated into reality—a little dirtier perhaps, and buzzing with flies—but none the less looking just like their ancient counterparts. Inside there is the same bridging of the centuries, with the guinea-pigs and babies grovelling in the half-light among a jumble of antique pots, basins, and vases decorated with the forms of llamas and birds, not to speak of the little *cochimilcos*—ancient idols which the babies used as dolls.

Then suddenly, just as you might well expect this half-dream to be carried on by the thin wailing of an antique flute, it is the sound of the radio which breaks into your reverie, while perched on a mound of mummies' winding cloths is a two-year-old child drinking his milk from a pre-Columbian gourd.

These are memorable sights for the traveller, and if he feels a twinge of remorse at buying some ancient piece of pottery for less than ten shillings, he can quickly console himself by the thought that Peru has enough treasure still underground to fill hundreds of museums for countless years to come. As Paul Morand writes: 'In Peru the really valuable mines are not the mines of gold or silver, but the tombs.' He goes on to substantiate this in his accounts of his fascinating discovery of the mummies of Pachacamac, the famous 'dead city' on the outskirts of Lima:

> There lie these mummies with their false heads, traces of which are to be found in all the museums of the world, bound like tortoises in their funeral bindings, rolled in their capes of yellow feathers, buried in cages or wells, enclosed in jars or funeral chambers—mummies dried up completely by the dehydrating air, carrying round their necks, as the Chinese did, parts of their bodies which had been mutilated in life. Mummies surrounded by clay models of their favourite birds or monkeys; mummies rolled in lacy shrouds, ancient bones lying scattered among unstrung turquoises, bracelets of gold supporting crumbling arms.
>
> There are mummies who lie beside their flutes, where they have lain for thousands of years—warriors, doubled up in their capes and holding their copper battle-axes. Subterranean races, spangled with gold, they find again in death their initial foetal position and lie there, in rows against a wall, exhausted travellers, crumbling like old cigars.

IX

THE SEVERED FOOT

We must not think, however, that the archaeologist discovers impressive pre-Columbian mummies at every spadeful. Sometimes he experiences unexpected disappointments, such as finding a parcel of cloth and bones wasted by the centuries, which disintegrates at the slightest touch.

One expert spent well over an hour unwrapping an oval bundle whose size and superb cloths had led him to believe that he had stumbled on some important personage. After unrolling layer upon layer of white cotton, there appeared at last a bag of black beans! This object undoubtedly represented the symbolic burial of some man who had disappeared without trace, perhaps a drowned man, or a missing warrior.

It often happens that a bundle contains only a fishing-net, a weapon, some teeth, a head resting on an earthenware vessel in the guise of a body, or a body without the head, for which a gourd is substituted.

These few examples show to what extent the archaeologist must beware of appearances, above all if he has to undertake the opening of a bundle in public, watched not only by the general public, experts and journalists, but even by cine-photographers for screen and television!

No matter what precautions are taken in the choice of the *fardo* (the immense bundle holding the sarcophagus), there is always the possibility of disappointment and even embarrassment. Dr. Jimenez-

Borja, who has more than once on being invited to open a *fardo* in public, decided to have radiographs of the chosen sarcophagus taken previously. This method has proved satisfactory hitherto, though even then there are liable to be surprises. The sarcophagus of the great Lord of Puruchucu, so photographed, led one to believe that inside there was a long silver or gold chain: in reality it turned out to be a splendid cape, embroidered on one side with thousands of silver sequins which resembled a coat of mail.

After the excavations of Walla-Marka it was decided to open the most promising *fardo* ever exhumed in Peru, before a public consisting of all the Peruvian and foreign experts in Lima. The funeral chamber where it was lying had already roused the interest of specialists because of its particularly well-designed construction. Six trunks of *guamo*, *chicle* tree, and *molle* (the sacred tree of the Incas) formed the outer support for an inner construction of wild reeds. There were great heaps of ceremonial Paraguayan tea, each packet wrapped for protection in a blue, white, and brown kerchief—numerous rods of bamboo painted all over with oil and wax—finely decorated sticks, the ends of which were burnt, indicating their probable use in pinning a roughly made weaving loom to the ground—work baskets and balls of weaving material made from fine reeds—and a little bag of lace. Everything pointed to this being a female mummy, and it was seriously hoped that it would be a Walla princess, possibly with considerable treasure enclosed.

Those who had been accustomed to this kind of find for many years agreed that it was an exceptional *fardo*, whose remarkable and uncommon shape would suggest that it dated from pre-Inca times. Four men were needed to move it, for it weighed about 300 pounds. Nothing quite like it had ever been seen. Long rolls of twisted cloth, as thick as an arm, formed a huge 'barrel' decorated with three multicoloured bags hanging from a tube-like belt, containing the customary magic seeds.

Dr. Jimenez-Borja organised a little museum in the exhibition hall of one of the large banks in Lima; here for a period of three weeks 'The Life of the First Inhabitants of San Isidro' could be seen. In the centre of the hall, well-lit and flanked on one side by the mummy of Puccla and on the other by Chinita, the sensational and mysterious *fardo* (not having a false head which would have permitted it a name) drew a crowd which would not normally have been at all interested in this kind of exhibition. From a show-case, masks grimaced at the curious who had been attracted by the High Priestess with the longest hair in the world. Hundreds of people from every social class in Lima filed silently past these ancestors who had been hitherto so ignored, and who, judging by the pottery, textiles, silver, jewellery, weapons, and baskets, had been great artists.

These three weeks seemed an eternity to us, for we were longing to penetrate the unknown interior of the *fardo*. On the day fixed for its opening we were in the first row in the Medical School at Lima. To reward the unusual interest shown by the public, the performance was, for the first time ever, to be televised from beginning to end.

If we were excited, the archaeologist and his team of experts were in a distinct state of agitation, for no one even knew for certain whether there was really a mummy inside the *fardo*!

The strained drawn faces of the radiologists, Dr. Jimenez-Borja's worried expression, the perplexed look of the assistants all dressed in white overalls as if for a serious operation (some carrying pads and pencils, others a ruler, a pen-holder, even a vacuum-cleaner) all surrounding the *fardo*, which was as tall as they, endowed the atmosphere with an air of almost unbearable tenseness.

Dr. Jimenez-Borja came forward at length to call for silence and the beads of sweat standing out on his forehead revealed something of what had happened: after having worked untiringly throughout the previous night, the two radiologists—at first surprised, then disconcerted, and finally discouraged—had told him that nothing at all appeared on the plates! The raised screen showed the anxious onlookers a series of absolutely emply plates; only the last showed a tiny speck right at the bottom of the *fardo*.

What were we to think? We exchanged questioning glances, for we had not forgotten the first fruitless attempts of photographers when the mummies had refused to reveal themselves on film.

Although obviously distressed, Dr. Jimenez-Borja began the opening ceremony: 'I wish you to maintain the deepest respect for the eternal sleep of the pre-Incan ancestor which this *fardo* represents,' he said. 'Nothing sensational should be expected; it is more probable that we shall find some treasure than an important scientific discovery.'

In the light of the floodlights which illuminated the side of the enormous sarcophagus bound in white cloth, the most extraordinary performance began—an extravagant strip-tease which was expected to bring to light, after many centuries of rest, some queen, princess, or vestal.

Under the three brown-and-white tapestry bags attached to the broad belt, a rose-brown band of cloth hid several layers of twisted material, which—when they were lifted—looked like great coiled snakes. Beneath these was an immense cotton cloth, not dissimilar, but arranged in pleats.

Dr. Jimenez-Borja drew the attention of all present to the immense care which had been taken in the making of this outer wrapping.

There followed a great length of material which measured sixty feet by thirty inches, and which hid the customary net of heavy cord, made from two strands of strong fibre forming a cage-like structure, through which three bamboos were threaded on either side—so supporting the whole. Right at the bottom we could make out a material decorated in a geometrical design; this was in turn protected by sixty feet of very fine gauze.

Under this appeared the first *cushma*, a tunic which covered the entire *fardo*, composed of two broad strips sewn together, the upper one being a brownish-pink and the lower one orange. This *cushma* reminded us vividly of the straight tunics of the Indian women belonging to certain tribes whose ethnography we had just been studying in the course of our expedition along the banks of the Ucayali and the Tamaya. In colour and shape it was particularly reminiscent of the ample shapeless tunic of the Campa Indians with openings for the head and arms.

'This,' explained Jimenez-Borja, 'indicates the influence of the people of the tropical forest regions over the old-established nations on the border of the Peruvian Pacific coast.'

This influence had already been brought to our attention in previous excavations by the agricultural tools and weapons of *chonta* wood, peculiar to the virgin forests but non-existent in the desert regions of the coast. It was illustrated in a concrete manner by the cloth mask of Chinita, which reproduced the savage Indian features with hair cut in a fringe that is so typical of women of the Amazon basin, and can also be seen in the current hair-style of the Mashi-guenga tribe, who live in the depths of the Urubamba jungles.

While the *cushma* was being carefully folded, we were told that it had not been woven as a garment, but specially for the purpose of binding the *fardo* in a perfectly fitting blanket.

Under this first *cushma* there appeared a second one, which we had already noticed owing to the geometric pattern we had seen at the bottom of the *fardo*. This pattern was not embroidered but hand-painted. In effect, two faces of cloth were stitched together and painted on either side. It was a valuable document, which might well typify the decorative themes created by the old inhabitants of the Rimac valley.

When the next layer (a closely fitting mesh) was unwrapped, it released so much fine dust that we were all enveloped in the white cloud! While the assistants struggled to take off their masks and everyone else spluttered, coughed, and rubbed their eyes, Dr. Jimenez-Borja showed his astonishment at finding so much sand and dust in such a fine *fardo*.

When we set to work again we found a large piece of white linen attached by long stitches, forming a design of crosses. Then count-less lengths of white linen, each one finer than the last, succeeded one another interminably; one of them contained some branches of the *guamo* tree.

Below the linen lay several lengths of twisted gauze, after which we came upon another layer of sand. The little mossy stones wound in with the rolls of cloth were a little puzzling, as it was clear that neither stones nor sand had found their way into the inside of the sarcophagus by accident, but had been put there on purpose. It was concluded that this was an example of an offering to the Pacha Mama, the much beloved and feared Mother Earth of ancient Peru—and even of modern Peru.

After this there appeared a greenish gauze, in whose folds we found balls of cotton, *guamo* leaves, Indian corn, and short strands of sewing thread.

At this point Dr. Jimenez-Borja, watch in hand, remarked that the operation had already taken half an hour, and that we would need at least as much time again to solve the mystery of the blank negatives. 'However,' he added more hopefully, 'we may suppose that all the sand and stones acted as a screen.'

Our hopes of finding a Walla princess were thus revived!

Next we detached a mesh, this time much more loosely bound round a white cloth and vertically striped in russet and brown. Unfortunately we found this much deteriorated, and thought sadly of the infinitely patient and tireless work put into it by weeping relatives and friends. All the evidence pointed to the fact that the mummy belonged to a high social rank, for an incredible number of weavers, spinners, cotton planters, and dressmakers must have been needed in the fabrication of all those wrappings.

We then found a beige material stained with what might have been blood, then another piece of material blackened with age, but which retained a small area of the original very beautiful blue colour. After this came a tunic with three broad dark stripes and a boat-neck firmly stitched on both sides with four tucks. With a sudden flash of humour Dr. Jimenez-Borja picked up the tunic, and draping it over his shoulders, demonstrated how the tunic could easily be made to slip off the shoulders of a coquette 'by mistake'. Certainly every-thing suggested a woman—the fine materials, the delicate designs, the shape of the tunic.

One by one the other lengths of cloth, netting, and tunics were removed, measured, numbered, and parcelled up. On the last tangle of vegetable net, we found little pots of maize attached to either side, and this maize was of a reddish purple colour similar to that of an under-ripe grape. This magic symbol caused a journalist to exclaim that the owner of the sarcophagus might be a *mazamorrera*, referring to those who even today in Peru prepare little pots of scented maize, a well-known speciality of Peru.

These heads of Indian corn were constantly being found, not always actually bound in with a mummy, but also in gourds filled with food offerings. It has been known for a long time that the ancient Peruvians were familiar with maize, signs of which are to be seen on many of the relics of ancient Peruvian culture. Maize probably formed the basis of the ancient Peruvian's larder.

A number of these hardened, shrivelled heads of corn—generally an amber yellow in colour—were found in Waka-Prieta, which is considered to be one of the oldest Peruvian pyramids in the north. On examination it was found that they were 2,700 years old, while in the south some maize was found that was over 3,000 years old.

The fact that this unusual type of maize was vitally linked to the life of the Wallas from Cuzco to Lima is seen, not only from the heads of corn buried in the tombs, but also even now, in the heart of the Sacred Valley not far from Cuzco, this sort of maize is still grown in an estate called Charcawalla. This particular maize has grains bigger than nuts, which pop when they burst.

This estate of Charcawalla, situated as it is in maize-growing country, has been selected as the centre of research into the possi-bility of production of this special maize on a commercial basis.

To return to the mysterious sarcophagus, the huge bundle of cloth, gauze, and coloured materials had now shrunk beyond recognition, and it was clear that it could not contain the mummy of an adult, but—at very most—a child.

It was all extremely odd! Dr. Jimenez-Borja looked decidedly puzzled as he withdrew a collection of little bamboo tubes, containing powder for the ceremony of tattooing. Each little tube was well stoppered with brown cotton.

Very little remained of the monumental cloth sarcophagus! Perspiration dripped from his brows, and his hand trembled as he bent over the remains of the pile of material. Was there nothing else? An exclamation of admiration from all present greeted the discovery of a remarkably vivid collection of parrot feathers sewn together and backed by fabric, a band of bright tourquoise feathers forming the border.

Forgetting his disillusionment for a moment, Dr. Jimenez-Borja exclaimed that such a valuable find proved beyond doubt the high social rank of this most honourable 'person'. He told us how these feathers must have been plundered from the coastal forest, and brought back across the Cordilleras—a tremendous feat—in order to produce such a magnificent garment.

We all remembered the legend of the Indian of the maritime Andes of Lima, who was so rich that his whole house and roof were covered with parrot feathers. The legend adds that these birds were found in numbers on the banks of the Pariachaka—a river of the Cordilleras.

A second robe of feathers—this time scarlet and yellow—seemed to bring the operation to an end. A puzzled silence pervaded the hall. Was there not even an idol, a precious stone—nothing? It was incredible.

The disillusionment of press, public, and technicians was quite obvious, when suddenly Dr. Jimenez-Borja plunged his hand into this last pile of feathers. His face lit up. What could it be?

It was a foot! A very tiny mummified foot—the twisted toes seeming to testify to its last painful reflex. It was the left foot of a young girl who cannot have been more than sixteen, of average height for her age, and it had almost certainly been severed during life.

This was all we were to know of the 'person' who had for so long intrigued us, and whom we might well have named 'The Cinderella of Sugar Loaf Mountain'.

*   *   *

What explanation could we give for this unexpected find? 'None for the moment,' concluded Dr. Jimenez-Borja.

Another incident came to his mind, however, and he duly related it to us, for in fact it was the only one that seemed to resemble the new mystery although it did not clarify it. Some months back a group of peasants from a nearby estate had found in the Valley of Chancay a sort of funeral chamber, made of four walls of flat stones piled upon each other. Inside there were eight little feet which looked as though they had belonged to adolescents of fifteen to eighteen years old. What barbaric rite demanded such sacrifices?

As for this foot so sumptuously wrapped and clothed that it weighed over 300 pounds, one can only suppose that it represented a symbolic burial, whose religious rites were of supreme importance.

*   *   *

Were there any other clues to the mystery? Our first summary search yielded poor results. At most we had discovered some traces which might point to human sacrifice among the pre-Columbians of Peru.

'All criminals, assassins, blasphemers, or those who were irreverent to the Incas were promised a cruel punishment'—so tells Huaman Poma, who goes on to say (as if he pardoned the practice), 'This involved a form of mutilation (the extremities such as the lips, nose, or ears were cut off) or blinding the victim so that he publicly showed his disgrace.' This terrifying custom was demonstrated by paintings on pottery, or embroidery, illustrating scenes where the heads and hands of the conquered were hung at the side of the road to be devoured by vultures.

In the course of excavation in the pyramids of Maranga at Lima, a shrunken head had been found hanging from the arm of a mummy, with shaven scalp and stuffed with straw.

Dr. Rebecca Carrion-Cachot believed that sacrifices were made only of arms and forearms, and not of any other parts of the body. Young girls without arms are depicted on the Huaylas' pottery, making religious offerings. Severed arms decorated with symbolic tattoos are to be seen on this same pottery.

In excavations which took place in Sacshuaman in 1933, Dr. Valcarcel had found two curious carved miniatures representing human feet artistically mounted on sea-shells. Could this also indicate the custom of partial sacrifice?

Writing in 1931, Tello reported: 'There are certain water vessels which depict with remarkable realism human arms and feet which had been amputated by a sharp stroke through the joint.'

Juan B. Lastres, in a remarkable study on Peruvian aborigine medicine, wrote in 1943: 'Amputations then practised have not left their trace on the actual bones but on the earthenware pots. Mutilated lips, nostrils, and feet—most commonly the left foot [like the one we had just discovered]—parts of the lower leg, these, according to Velez Lopez, were recognised mutilations for punishment—the punishment always being suited to the crime.'

But we had still discovered nothing concrete about out particular foot. Accident, punishment, crime, sacrifice? Our Cinderella of Walla-Marka, was she perhaps devoured by the pumas who came down into the valleys at the foot of the Andes at certain seasons of the year? Or perhaps, as someone suggested on seeing the design of serpents on the material in the sarcophagus, she may have been swallowed by some huge water-snake?

The mystery remains.

X

THE PYRAMID VALLEY
WHEN THE PIZARROS ARRIVED

We are still quite uncertain what language was spoken when the five Pizarros discovered the Lima Valley. It might have been Aymara, which was spoken in the high plateaux at that time, remnants of which are found in the place-names around Lima today. It might have been the Cauqui dialect heard by Hernando Pizarro on the road to the Pachacamac sanctuary and still spoken at Tupe, in the mountains above Lima. Or Mochica, recognised by Father Barnaby Cobo on his way to Carawalla, on the outskirts of the recently founded Spanish capital. Fortunately Father Cobo recorded his impressions of this new and strange land, and has left information which is useful, if incomplete:

> Before the Spaniards arrived in this land, the valley and surrounding region was densely populated by Indians. We have found traces of many tribes living there, all speaking different languages, and have noticed that the inhabitants of Carawalla and the surrounding territory spoke a language which was also spoken towards Chancay and the north. In the region between Carawalla and Pachacamac, however, there lived another nation.

And here he enigmatically stops. His statement that various tribes lived in the valley is confirmed by other chroniclers:

> The Indians wore head-dresses by which they were easily identifiable. If they were Yungas they wore their hair like gypsies, and they dressed differently in each province.

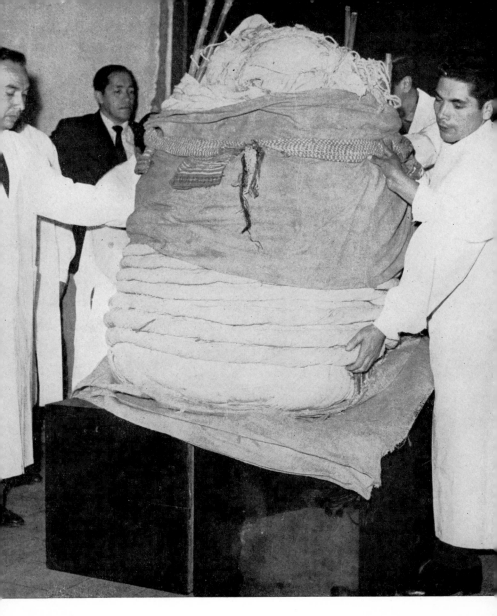

Dr. Jimenez-Borja at the unveiling of the huge funeral *fardo*, containing the mysterious severed foot. This sarcophagus, made up of lengths of cotton about sixty feet long and three feet wide, weighed more than three hundred pounds.

PLATE IX

Nevertheless, as we are going to see more and more clearly, the Wallas held an important position among these various tribes and nations. We find them appearing time and again in the cloak-and-dagger exploits and wild treasure hunts of the Pizarros. For example Hernando Pizarro, returning from the northern lands of the Chimus, enters 'a beautiful valley of maize plantations, divided by a thunderous torrent', and here, in the village of Walla-Marka, he rested for forty-eight hours and was entertained by Pumapacha, the lord of the district, while his horses recovered, exhausted by their hard journey.

When Hernando and his men were descending the high valleys to the coast near Lima, they came upon the Ata-Wallas (or Atawillos) —a Walla clan who delighted the Spaniards both by their taste and ingenuity, as well as by the ardour with which they set themselves to their task of cultivating the most unyielding soil with patience and intelligence.

Francisco Pizarro, the famous Inca conqueror, was quick to see the value attached to 'one of the most perfect lands in which to spend a life', namely the land of the Ata-Wallas, and did not hesitate to ask Charles V for the title of Marquis of the Atawillos, together with

PLATE X

The Sugar Loaf *Waka* after the work of restoration. The face of the pyramid is made up of fifty terraces of sun-dried mud bricks conical in form, looking rather like grains of corn. The primitive form of construction leads us to place this pyramid among the oldest in Lima, and it may even be the oldest of all, dating back two or three thousand years.

G

twenty thousand Indian subjects for himself and his descendants, and the taxes and tributes due from the province, in return for services rendered to the Spanish Crown during the conquest of Peru.

He duly received his title, but in response to his more material demands the Emperor stated that he himself would make a survey of the land, in case the gift might give rise to envy. Whether Pizarro ever received it or not remains a mystery, but there are several old documents which mention that he had twenty thousand Indians as slaves. It is also mentioned that one of his relatives became owner of the Carawalla estate which stands at the gates of Lima, and that Puruchucu (its ruler) and his palace were given to Miguel de Estete.

When the Pizarros arrived in the Lima valley they found that although it was included in the northernmost of the four regions which made up the Inca empire (Tahuantinsuyo), it was still being run on the feudal system practised a hundred years earlier by the former inhabitants of the coast. The Incas had simply divided the people into three groups or *hunus* of ten thousand families each, each one of which was governed by an Inca ruler (the *hunukamayoc*), to whom both the Walla *kurakas* and the Inca *regulos* were subject.

A *tocricuc* (controller) was elected by the Incas as head of these confederations, whose political, civil, military, and religious organisation was surprisingly advanced: every *tocricuc* was almost completely independent of his neighbour, and lived in a castle, built invariably on top of one of the ancient *wakas*.

Carawalla was the principal town of the first *hunu* (region); Maranga, in the centre of the valley, was the second, and the third was Surco.

Thus the valley of Lima had a population, according to chroniclers, of about 120,000 to 150,000 inhabitants of various races, who were later to become the inhabitants of Lima: a mixed race which was later to have the noble blood of the Spanish *hidalgos* added to it.

Having rejected Jauja in the Cordilleras as being too far from the sea to make a good capital of Peru, it was found that the heart of the

Rimac valley afforded the spot best sheltered from the coast; and it was here that the great conqueror sent his explorers with instructions to recommend the best possible spot for a capital city.

Let us imagine ourselves with these explorers of the past. What would we see? Where exactly was the village of the 'Lord of Lima'? In which palace did he live? The historical details are patchy and blurred and we must content ourselves with what little we know.

Crossing the suspension bridge which connects the Rimac valley to that of Carawalla, and taking the old road coming from the far northern Chan-Chan, capital of the Chimus (which for long centuries has acted as footpath for pilgrims on their way to the imposing villa-sanctuary of Pachacamac), we may imagine three bearded horsemen astride their travel-worn beasts, weighed down by their heavy arms, coming at last upon the green oasis near the mouth of the river Rimac.

In the burning sun of the summer season which in this latitude reigns in January, Pizarro's envoys could make out numerous truncated pyramids, painted yellow or red, and numerous magnificent murals on the palaces and fortifications.

These monumental constructions which through the centuries have transformed the coastal plain into a line of pyramids must then have been a most impressive sight.

Four *tambos* (stone posting-houses) defended the exits—Tambo Inga, Makaat, Lima Tambo, and Irmatambo, of which there still exist remains. Arms, clothing, and provisions were available from these *tambos*. Among these Incan relics were scattered native villages of sand-coloured *adobe*. These stretched over the sides of the denuded grey Andes down to the sea, and a great back-cloth was provided by the soaring peaks above.

The network of little irrigation canals twisted in and out of the plots of cultivated ground, which in turn were surrounded by walls of pressed sand or stones similar to those used in building the dwellings. It was this system of irrigation which the Spaniards most admired, and which made Hernando Pizarro exclaim: 'These people live by irrigation'—a fact which is indeed impressive after coming through so much desert land.

Another factor which surprised and delighted Pizarro and his colleagues was the abundance of orchards and trees: 'All was a great forest of fruit trees', they wrote on first entering Lima. Alas, one must add that none of these trees remains today.

The whole territory was defended by tall citadels surrounded by moats, bastions, and parapets, built in the same earth *adobe* to protect the population from possible invasion through the deep gorges which cleft the mountain chain.

Sacred villas, sanctuaries, sports grounds, and high theatre platforms could be distinguished, surrounded by huge, ochre-coloured walls. Some decorations in relief were found, usually of a mythological or warlike nature, sometimes pools of fish or arbours of birds, or geometrical designs like those we had found on tapestries.

Lima was at this time at once rustic, mystic, and maritime; this last attribute was supplied by the two little gondola ports; the gondolas were made of woven reeds, and men rode astride them a little like the *caballitos de totora* (little reed horses) which one can see today only in the port of Huanchaco, some 300 miles to the north of Lima, and which are often represented on the pottery of that period. On the site of the two fishing-harbours, the straggling ports of Chorillos and Callao were later established. The bay of Callao was soon to see Spanish *caravellas* anchoring, ready to swell their holds with gold and pre-Columbian treasure, making it a notorious spot for brigands and pirates before it became one of the largest merchant ports of the South Pacific.

It was into a scene of calm sea, disciplined oasis kept trim by the aborigines, and encircled by desert screened off by the mountain range (an impressive scene even to a European of today) that the *conquistadores* advanced at a trot, passing the Indian planters who were afraid of these unknown beasts who carried 'men of iron', who were said to feed on gold.

How did these natives live in 1533? It is difficult to build up a clear picture from the accounts of the chroniclers of the time, as their opinions vary greatly. Alonzo Enriquez, travelling up the whole Peruvian coast in 1534, reports that 'the people had houses made only of bamboo, similar to hen-houses and just as dirty and as badly kept'.

Ten years later they were described as living in even worse conditions, under trees or in the shelter of the undergrowth, while Cieza de Leon describes them in 1548 in their large *adobe* houses, shaded from the sun by shelters of rush matting.

One is led to believe that certain chroniclers were influenced in their description by the scorn in which the Yungas of the coast were held by the Inca officials, who considered them:

> people of little worth; neither good at governing nor waging war;
> poor in gold and silver—that which they had being gained in exchange
> for fish and fruit; cotton-clad and eaters of raw or cooked maize,
> and half-raw meat.

The Spaniards on the other hand, amazed by what they had seen in the mountains and avid for the treasures of the Incas, neglected these civilisations of the sands. When building the Cuidad de los Reyes on the site of the village of Lima, however, the Spaniards adopted—with elaborations—the architecture used by the ancient Peruvians, which was so well adapted to their peculiar climatic conditions; modern Lima still bears witness to this architecture in the typical old-style balcony houses, usually found at the juncture of two roads, whose walls are invariably coated with bamboo and mud and whose roofs are made of plaited reeds.

★　　★　　★

The state of the *wakas* at that time is very problematical. Now rediscovered and brought back to life by the magic touch of the archaeologist, it is doubtful whether they were being used at the time of colonisation, for the chroniclers constantly refer to them as 'artificial hills'. Some centres must, however, have been found in very good condition—among them the large Maranga pyramid.

The urban centre of Irmatambo-Surco, built on the sides of an enormous rock, must also have been in almost perfect condition. It was on this rock—the *Morro Solar*—that Bernardo Pizarro was received by the great *Kuraka* of Pachacamac (or Triamchumbi) and ate a princely breakfast in the palace described by Father Cobo:

> The houses owned by the *Kuraka* have various figures painted on their walls, and there is one very luxurious *waka* or temple, and many other buildings which are complete but for their roofs.

Where, we wonder, was the village of Lima situated in this Peruvian Babylon? This is one of the hardest to solve of our many enigmas, for most of the chroniclers of the time refer to the village without giving a clue to its precise location. Cobo, for example, tells us that the village of Lima was near Maranga, that it covered over a square mile, and was to be found 'near the temple of the god Rimac, the oracle of the region'—all of which is not very helpful! Father Calencha is not much more explicit:

> From Lima-Tambo to Marengo there is a series of houses or palaces, one belonging to the Inca king and the others to the dignitaries of the village. On the south bank of the Rimac river there is a building which, with the lands around it, belongs to the ruler of Lima.

As for Cieza de Leon, generally so long-winded in his descriptions, he hardly gives any space to this problem, saying only that the site was located 'in a flat part of this valley, two little leagues from the sea'. None the less, in spite of their vagueness, all these slight clues do lead us in the direction of the Cerro San Cristabel, where today a great luminous cross shines into the night sky of 'Gran Lima', as though studded with diamonds. Modern Lima was in fact brought into being about this time by Francisco Pizarro.

There, in a short reign of glory, he built his palace on the foundation of a *waka* on the corner of the vast quadrangle of the Plaza de Armas. Opposite this, built on the site of the *waka* where Tauli-chusco (the last little Walla king) had his palace, was the Spanish cathedral where the great Pizarro himself, murdered a bare six months later by one of his old companions, slept his last sleep in a glass sarcophagus. Thus embalmed, Pizarro's mummy makes a sad sight with its shrivelled head as red as an old leather belt, fixed to the body by a piece of wire!

Pizarro first decided to found his capital where it now stands when, on the 18th of January 1535, he received the account of six days' exploration of the coastal valley undertaken by Ruiz Diaz, Juan Tello de Guzman, and Alonso Martin de don Benito. His messengers had already recommended it as being 'well provided with water, wood, and other things necessary for a republic'; they also judged it a healthy place.

What remains of this village? Almost nothing at all, except the crumbling ruins of *wakas* and palaces, or the last remaining fragments of the old earth flagstones which can be seen almost at the mouth of the river in the oldest and most picturesque part of Lima.

Despite our inability to be certain of the exact boundary lines of Inca Lima, we can nevertheless outline the three larger fiefs which made up the post-Inca valley of Rimac, and which were at the time but grains of sand in the gigantic empire of Tahuantinsuyo.

Taking both ancient and modern documentary evidence into account, we can see that there was a village of Taulichusco to the north of the present town of the same name, which was governed by the *kuraka* of the village of Lima until 1535, when it became known as Piti-Piti, the seaport of Maranga, before finally becoming our modern Callao. It is not known whether these small townships now lying in ruins at the foot of the Andes were all quite independent of each other or whether they were grouped together under the rule of little kings whose names are not mentioned by the chroniclers.

★   ★   ★

It was the historian Porras Barrenchea who made one of the most important discoveries about the ancient inhabitants of the Peruvian capital when he found an official report conserved in the Las Indias

archives which contained the information that Taulichusco, the great
lord of the valley who knew Pizarro, was extremely old at the time
of the Spaniards' arrival, having been in power since the days of the
Inca Huayna Kapak. We learn more about the spread of Taulichusco's power, and also about the way the Incas chose the people
who were to rule under them, when we are told that before becoming overlord of the Rimac valley, Taulichusco (descendant of the
Cuzco Wallas) had been the 'servant' of Mama Vilo, Huayna
Kapak's wife.

Thanks to this document we were able to make sense of several
clues whose relationship had been puzzling us during the course of
our investigations: firstly the appearance of the word 'servant' linked
to the names of several of the Cuzco Wallas, and secondly the rather
puzzling relationship indicated by this word between Inca and
Walla. It now seemed fairly certain that after their quarrels over the
land were settled the Inca-Walla relationship was one of master and
highly trusted advisor, rather than that of master-servant. This
theory was supported by the account given in the same document
of Cassapaxxa, Taulichusco's brother, 'accompanying the Inca king
all around the court'. Their father, who was conquered and protected by this same king, must also have ruled over some part of the
valley, as the document describes him as fighting against rival
neighbouring tribes of which one, the Colli, invaded the Rimac
valley in force.

Because of his age, however, Taulichusco had delegated most of
his power to his son Guachinamo when the Pizarros arrived.
Guachinamo always appeared before the Spaniards with an impressive retinue. Like his ancestors, he lived in the Chayacalca palace in
the Walla valley.

His brother, who succeeded him under a Spanish name (Don
Gonzalo), spent his reign trying to abolish idolatry amongst the
Wallas in his region. Soon, however, most of them dispersed,
becoming servants of the *conquistadores*, or escaping and becoming
vagabonds. Don Gonzalo soon realised that he was in the process

of losing all his followers, for the Spaniards had taken over their hereditary estates, and were destroying property and fruit trees in order to build Spanish houses. Guavas and sweet potatoes were the Indians' main source of food, and the Spanish ruthlessness threatened them with extinction. As a result of these abuses, the venerable Taulichusco came in person before the Spanish governor to protest, and in the course of a memorable dialogue he was heard to say to Pizarro:

and where can the Indians multiply if their lands are taken from them?

to which the Pizarro replied:

We have no other possible choice of place for our town.

It was but a few paces from the spot at which these words were spoken that Taulichusco himself was destined to disappear in 1594, together with his *kuraka* (Puccla Cassa) and the *kuraka* of Surco (Tantachacumbe), both reduced to unhappy skeletons by being forced to teach music in order to survive.

★   ★   ★

By 1687 the site of this ancient Walla village had become a pleasant country resort of ranches and farms. Spanish nobles spent a pleasant and healthy time convalescing there; an Italian built a bar and a marquis a 'crystal palace'. It was a beautiful place, close to the sea yet protected by three high sandy cliffs, and so overgrown with flowers that it was named Miraflores, a name it keeps to this day as one of Lima's most wealthy residential areas.

It was in this calm suburb, witness of so much past grandeur, that Don Esteban Calla (a descendant of the Wallas) was honoured by the Inca title of *kipukamayoc* at the end of the seventeenth century. If he could no longer boast of keeping the Inca accounts, he was at least Poet Laureate of his state.

A hundred years later Felix Camlla, a great Indian, became mayor of Miraflores, the place which had been the grandeur and decadence of his own ancestors. Although apparently completely Spanish, Lima has an Indian root, for it springs directly from the Wallas. The very name Lima was preferred to the other name (Cuidad de los Reyes) because of its Indian root, although Pizarro had originally intended the latter.

XI

WAKOTO, THE WAY OF THE SOULS

Like Egypt, Babylon and China, ancient Peru lived in un-
interrupted communication with a magic world which was
in total harmony with the world of reality.

LUIS E. VALCAREL

Let us now take the legendary Wakoto, the 'way of the souls',
the sad 'path of silence' followed by the ancient Peruvians
and by their present-day descendants.

To do this, we shall leave Lima and travel for a while up the road
to the Andes, which carries us to a height of 10,000 feet into the
jagged mountain range of La Viuda, where we can see the monumental ruins of the 'lost cities' of the Ata-Wallas. We shall almost
certainly be unaccompanied in our wanderings, for it is rare for
travellers to visit these gloomy peaks today, despite the fact that this
is one of the oldest pre-Columbian roads.

If, however, we have the luck to meet some shepherd watching
his flock of llamas in these desolate regions, the chances are that he
will draw our attention to a strange rock, the centre of which is
hollowed out to make a ring, encircling a patch of sky. This is the
sacred rock of Wakoto, the final goal, the resting-place of souls.

The pre-Inca road starts from the ancient Inca relay-station of
Pariak, which is in the heart of the mountain range, at the junction
of several tracks, each coming up from the Pacific coast. The whole
region abounds in vast caverns and underground galleries, situated
at an altitude of between nine and twelve thousand feet. Broken
pieces of pottery and the remains of cooking-utensils prove that they
were once inhabited by a cave-dwelling people.

Most of the Indians of today, however, refuse to guide us. In fact they believe that these *wakas* are still haunted and that no human being entering them can come out alive. So strong is this belief that on one occasion when two Indians did in fact dare to penetrate the precincts, one of them died immediately afterwards of a nervous illness springing directly from this inborn fear.

Some of these caves, such as the cave of Wallocuay on the Manko glacier, were used for the offering of the Ata-Wallas' sacrifices; and one can still see, at the furthest end of the grotto, a single-pillared alter leading to the caverns where the sacrificed victims were thrown, after their blood had flowed into the great stone basins which still stand there today.

★　　★　　★

The path leads us over the tops of the peaks, all of which are sacred to the Apachota Indians of the region, and then through the *apachotas* (high pasture-lands) across the glaciers to the pre-Columbian farms, past the villages and peaceful lagoons reflecting the ever-changing colour of the sky, past the famous glacier of Manko Kapak, until finally we arrive at the immense grazing grounds of llamas. These may remind us of the Inca legend in which Anko, son of Wallanaku, and his descendants are made responsible for the up-bringing of the imperial llamas.

When an Ata-Walla died, it was believed that his spirit had to follow this same agonising sky-bound path which leads to the *waka* of Wakoto, and it is very likely that our Indian guide will think we are accompanying the soul of some recently deceased villager, to watch it being subjected to the two ritual tests. Indeed, if we question him, he will describe in such faithful detail the wandering soul which has come from some tiny hamlet in the vicinity that we shall be quite taken aback by the vividness of the account.

If the soul is masculine it will travel sadly, its back bent like the back of our guide under the constant load of its earthly possessions, among which is always numbered a *takkla* or primitive spade which it must carry in its hand.

If the soul is feminine it will carry its distaff or loom, just like the Indian women who cross our path from time to time.

All souls pause at the last bend in the road from which its native village may be seen in order to bid farewell to their people with a mighty cry which reverberates around the steep mountain slopes. This cry is the Antewakay hymn, the act of taking leave of the sun and of life to enter the darkness of eternal night.

Here and there the soul will stop, weighed down with sadness. At length, leaving the populated area, it will travel through glacial and deserted regions until it reaches the stopping-place called Kakawayschuko, where it must make some offering and undergo the first test—part of the magic rites of the *aukis*, the ancestral spirits of the mountains.

The masculine souls must then prove skill of arm by slinging a stone on to a sacred ledge some hundred yards away, and our guide drew our attention to innumerable stones scattered along this ledge. Happy the skilful soul who then continues its ascent to the summit of Wakoto, but unhappy the soul whose aim proved vain, for this is a fatal proof of laziness, lack of courage, or of wrong-doing in life.

The female soul, her back bent under the traditional striped *kepi* in which she has carried her babies and possessions throughout her lifetime, must sit on a boulder and spin a fabric which will be the symbol of her past life. The soul's memory will weave into the fabric the sum of all her actions, good and bad. If her life has been full of goodness and courage, the material will be soft and the threads lustrous and bright, of all the colours of the rainbow; but if her bad deeds have outnumbered the good, the material will unwind itself and her soul will be hurled into the shadowy Umay-Nany—the land of suffering.

We followed the path of the souls who had passed their first test, and continued on our way up the steep glacial moraine. Eventually we reached Mutte, the site of a pre-Inca property where

the souls pause to sing a lament. Our guide claimed to have heard
these voices frequently and his belief in the journey of the souls was
unshakable.

At last, relieved of their burden and joyful at the sight of the little
village of Huacramata, the souls will intone the gay *ayri* (a wild
masculine song) or the sweet *yarawi* (sung by the female souls alone).
Carefree dances help them to forget all their regret for life and for all
that they loved on earth; they have now drunk of the shining water
of Kon-Yaku, the water of forgetfulness of the god Kon, who is
personified in the shape of a little stream which flows over limestone,
thus whitening its water and giving it an alkaline taste which the
Indian considers purifying.

Arriving at the foot of the sacred Wakoto, the good souls will
undergo the second and last test. Here the path is blocked by two
rocks rising from a broad common base: the higher rock is the men's,
and the lower is the women's rock. Each has a gaping hole through
the centre.

The soul will then take up the *takkla* and present itself resolutely
before the narrow aperture in the rock. If it has really been virtuous
and brave and just during life, it will—despite the extreme narrow-
ness of the hole—pass without harm through the 'gate of eternity',
just as in life it has been able to conquer hardships, privations, and
other human sufferings. If not it will remain there, invisible but
forever fixed before the Wakoto.

But the souls who pass safely through to the other side will
experience the joy and immortality of the gods on the glacier of
Manko.

In the province of Huarochiri, on the outskirts of the little Andes
town of Laraos, one can see a similar 'chapel' as well as the sacred male
and female rocks, at the end of another 'pathway of souls' which is
reached by a stairway cut deeply into the granite. These traditions,
which are still very much alive, demonstrate a remarkably clear
sense of moral justice—a feeling which continues to influence the
life of the Indian today in a very powerful way.

The chronicler Huaman Poma tells us that at the time of the Incas the spirits of the mad or the wicked wandered freely among the people of Chinchaysuyo, joining with other *suyos* at Aullaypampa where they suffered thirst, heat, fire or cold together. This underground world—the equivalent of our hell—was for the pre-Columbian Indians the dwelling place of the demon Supay, and its name was Ukupacha Supaypa Wacin.

Another tradition tells us that the souls of Incas went straight to the sun, father of the dynasty, while the souls of 'upstarts' went to Hanac Pacha, and the souls of the lower orders to the celestial space nearest the earth.

★   ★   ★

The Indians of the Cordillera and the valleys of Paucartambo— from where Tello supposes the Wallas originated—maintain even today a strange funeral custom: at three in the morning the family and the friends of the dead man meet together in front of the tomb to sing the *yunka*—a sort of hymn to the virgin forest, which one can see covering the base of the mountains like a great green ocean. It is their belief that the souls of their people go to Hatun Yunka— the Great Jungle. This is the song we can hear resounding through the dark Andean night:

> Where are you going, my Father?
> I am going to the Great Jungle—I am going to walk there.
> What will you do there? Who will take you?
> I shall gather the sweet *coca*, and I shall go by myself.
> Return soon, return soon,
> I shall await you weeping,
> I shall await you mourning.

We shall stop again in the sacred valley of Urubamba, where there are still some Indians of Walla origin, and where the beliefs in the after-life are still very much alive.

The soul is like the wind. One can neither see nor touch it, but one can feel it. It is an invisible being with wings, which has its home in the body from birth, and which can leave the body temporarily if an *auki* (a spirit of the Andes) so decides.

Mummies, here called *sok'a,* are not dead people but individuals who never die because of their great wisdom and whose spirits can make a brief appearance and emerge from their caverns during magic ceremonies.

After death, the soul lives for eight days with its own people, before undertaking the great journey which will be the reflection of its past life. Its path takes it across the river Cuzco, then in the direction of Angostura towards Hurk an Mayu, the fast-flowing river on whose bank live the spirits of dogs. The heaven of the good souls is on the opposite bank, which they will reach by riding a dog across.

Once this bank is reached, a wide path leads to a fertile paradise where water and crops abound, and where the good people dwell. The spirits of thieves and adulterers wander around frightening

PLATE XI

(*Top*). Detail of the poker-work designs decorating the ceremonial dishes. On the bottom of the wooden vase on the left there appeared a curious little sign; was it the 'signature' of the artist, the mark of the owner, or perhaps one of the letters of a mysterious alphabet?

(*Foot*). Its expression fixed for ever, the mask of the White Wizard appears before us, at night, like a ghost.

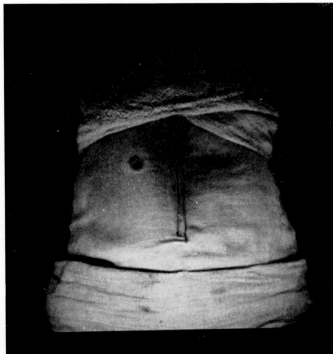

people, making them ill, turning drinks and food bad, and maltreating the dogs which had helped the good souls across the river.

Stranger still are current beliefs regarding children's souls. Those who have not been baptised go to Llimpu—a dark place where they carry on a desperate search for the clapper of a bell. The day on which one of them finds this and rings the bell will mark the Last Judgment. The spirits of men can then live again on the earth, naked and flying from branch to branch, nourishing themselves on fruit like birds.

All the dead man's clothes must be meticulously washed, or he will return to claim any missing garment. One week after death, friends and family help in the washing and it becomes a sort of ceremonial picnic.

Another curious custom is that of watering the tomb with holy water poured from human skulls. The Huaynos, who have the gayest funeral customs, sing a sort of 'departure chant' named *kachapariy*, and the distribution of fermented *chicha* served in a gourd passed from one to the other is extremely generous, while at the stroke of midnight the virtues of the deceased are lauded by friends and relatives, who sit around chewing green *coca* leaves.

★   ★   ★

Plate XII

Pottery container in the shape of a parrot, dating from the end of the Tiahuanaco culture.

Container in the shape of a frog from the Marango culture.

H

It is interesting to note a certain similarity between the Peruvian 'path of souls' and its equivalent in other ancient civilisations. In the fourth Egyptian dynasty we find the symbol of the 'eternal path', the narrow gate, the 'Ra' through which the soul must pass on its way to the dark shades.

In China it is the *Yunpi*, 'the wall of ghosts', which replaces the Peruvian *Wakoto* and the Egyptian *Ra*. The Chinese soul must, by dint of wisdom, find the narrow slit made invisible under many concealing layers, where Tao is to be found.

⋆   ⋆   ⋆

There must be countless paths of souls in Peru. Eighty miles north of Lima we found another near the little gate of Huancho, still quite colonial in appearance, where numerous ruins of *wakas* can be seen. The fishermen there told us that the souls of their ancestors issued from the temple, which was previously situated on top of one of the *wakas*. These souls are said to forgather on the *isla de las animas*, directly opposite the bay of Carquin, where they were conducted by a sea-lion.

To the south of Lima, fishermen told us that souls were protected by petrified goddesses, whose silhouettes they showed us—some grey islets formed entirely of lava, whose guano-whitened summits form the only landmarks in an otherwise featureless ocean. We were told, moreover, that in order to reach *Upa Marka* (The Dumb Land) the souls must cross a river by a suspension bridge made from very fine human hair, and that they are helped in this perilous crossing by black dogs.

From time to time a soul will visit the mainland from these islands, and will invariably herald its approach by inciting the natural elements, so that a strong wind blows off the Pacific, a strange cloud appears in the sky, or rain falls.

For the Chimus of the north—who depend on the sea for a living —Kon was the ancestral soul of their creator. It was Kon who sent rain unexpectedly in the dry season. Tradition explains that the deserts near the coastal strip came into being because the Chimus had offended Kon, who punished them by withholding rain.

XII

THE FAMOUS TALKING ORACLE OF RIMAC

One of the greatest mysteries connected with the *wakas* and the history of the Wallas is the problem of substantiating the exact place where the famous oracle was heard—the talking idol of Rimac. It was consulted by people from all down the coastline, and was adopted by the Incas.

Once again we can only reproach the chroniclers of the time of the conquest who do little else but arouse our curiosity. Here, for example, is what Father Calancha writes:

> Apart from the great temple and *waka* of the supreme Pachacamac, every valley had its own particular god. That of the neighbouring valley was the god Rimac, whose temple and *waka* can be seen today at Chacra de Rimac Tampu, the Dominican farm. The village nearby spread itself over half a league. There can be found not only the place where the famous talking idol had its abode, but also the village known by the misleading name of Lima, before the foundation of Cuidad de los Reyes. In the same way that Rimac (mispronounced by the Spaniards) has become Lima, Rimac Tampu has become Limatambo which means the house of he who speaks.

These explanations are not made any more helpful by the fact that Lima has altered radically since the conquest, and the Dominican farm has disappeared without trace.

At the end of last century Raimondi claimed that it may have been near Lima, on the road to Chorillas. This area is now occupied by one of the most modern airports in South America, and several of the chroniclers of the conquest would have agreed with this. One chronicler, however, wrote that the talking idol was situated in a *mochadero* very near the *cacique's* residence.

Which *cacique* did he mean? Was he referring to Taulichuso, lord of the settlement of Lima? Or to Puccla Casa, Kuraka of Chaycalca? There are various possibilities but perhaps Taulichuso is the most likely, as various documents of the conquest refer to the oracle being beside the river, and undoubtedly Taulichuso's dwelling was beside the river.

It is to this view that Dr. Quesada inclines in his recent book on Lima, where he writes:

> The *wakas* were numerous (one doesn't know whether friends or rivals) and situated at various points within the valley. There was one, however, whose exact position has never been substantiated (Lima-tambo, Maranga, Wadma—at any rate somewhere near the river). It was the principal oracle of the district, and became the meeting-place of those who wished to know the voice of destiny, the sanc-tuary which spread its other-worldly cloak of mystery and legend over this otherwise unromantic stretch of coast.

But if the idol spoke at Limatambo it was not near the river, and if, on the contrary, it was heard on the banks of the river, it could not have spoken in the immense religious centre of the Wallas, the *Waka* Pucclana, which is a reasonable conclusion if we take the '*cacique's* residence' to refer to Surco, owner of this enormous *waka*, the biggest in the whole Rimac valley.

Father Cobo, the great historian of the first years of colonisation, supports the claim that this was the *waka* in question. He goes on to explain that two and a half centuries before the Incas conquered the coastal strip the Wallas had 'worshipped in a place which was called Walla, in a *waka* called Pucclana, *where there was an oracle of great renown throughout the whole coast*'.

This leads inevitably to the conclusion that if one of the great oracles of the region was the well-known oracle of Pachacamac, the other can only be the equally famous one from Rimac—not so near the river as several people have imagined, but closely connected with the Wallas, whose talking divinity it became.

The *Waka* Pucclana (or Juliana), situated at a short distance from the 'Sugar Loaf', leads us into the heart of this Walla valley, where the modern suburbs of Miraflores and San Isidro mark the bounds of the city. Here we can still admire this colossal *waka* the exterior of which originally covered two-thirds of a square mile, modelled on pre-Inca pyramids of Pachacamac, rectangular in shape. The ancient Peruvians arranged the clay bricks like books on a bookshelf, vertical and horizontal rows alternating. Apart from the pyramid of Walla Marka all the *wakas* in Lima are built in the same way. Between the rows of *adobe* in the ancient city of Maranga, mummified children have been found alongside dogs and guinea-pigs, generally buried in pairs.

While Carlos Romero and Max Uhle were excavating the *Waka* Pucclana, it was found that the *mochadero* (or place of worship) measured over 300 yards in length, 70 in width, and 35 in height. They made a very interesting discovery in the course of their excavations: a speaking-tube ran the whole length of the *waka*, its mouth forming a terrace which itself was over thirty yards long. Those faithful to the mystery cult used to place their offerings to the idol in this spot—very often great bowls of *chicha*. At the back of the *waka* was the aperture where the speaking idol was concealed awaiting the questions of the faithful, and replying to them through the ingenious tube.

After this discovery, it was suspected that Rimac Tampu or Limatambo (the temple of the one who speaks) could well have been quite simply the largest and most famous one—the *Waka* Pucclana or Juliana. Thus the problem seemed to be resolved and we might have been justified in assuring that the temple of Rimac-Tampu and the *Waka* Pucclana of the Wallas were one and the same thing (adducing as additional proof an authentic document dated 1560 which confirmed that 'the demon in *Waka* Juliana spoke through a hole') were it not for the fact that all the *wakas* possess underground galleries, some of which are of exquisite workmanship. Probably all the *wakas* had oracles to whom the Indians gave offerings, listening to the prognostications given through the priests of this strange cult.

The Incas also had their *waka*-oracles. Among the most famous of these figures Anko-Kawa, whose name suggests that this idol also could have well been a Walla! There are also various references to an oracle who replied from the trunk of a tree; when the Spaniards felled the tree, a parrot emerged from the severed trunk.

Some years ago an underground entrance was discovered to another *waka* situated in the Rimac valley, on the lands of the *Kuraka* of Chayacalca. This is the *Waka* Orbea, between Magdalena Vieja and Magdalena Nueva, very near the ruins of the 'sacred towns' Wadka and Maranga. It has been suggested that the underground gallery of Orbea might well have been used as a speaking-tube by an oracular priest.

This *waka* served a *hunu* or group of ten thousand families, who lived in little townships of artificial hills, a series of temples, houses, and a multitude of little palaces, which were accessible through three entrances, all of which led into zigzag labyrinths and were closed at night by skins of beasts or by planks.

Middendorf claims the town of Wadka as the home of the Rimac oracle—'the idol with the human face', whom he associates with the god of wind, about whom Oviedo gives us some further information:

> At some five hundred spots along the coast one can see temples situated on high ground with stone or wood idols. The most noble god was Wat'an, 'the Whirlwind', though according to Father Cobo, Watan is only the deformed name of *wadka*, the pyramid on which the celibate priests (dressed in white with mitres on their heads) carried out sacrifices after undergoing a rigorous fast. They would tear out the hearts of their victims, to offer them to their god.

A 'triumphal path' was walled in by *adobe* flagstones on which faces were painted—possibly gold masks of the sort worn during festivities, warriors on the run, fish, lizards, or scorpions which were repainted whenever the weather threatened to destroy them.

Perhaps the wind oracle was too demanding in his sacrifices, and not always of good faith; it is interesting to note that the *quechua* word *wateka* (derived from *wadka*) denotes a bad counsellor, or a false and tempting demon. There seems to be little doubt that the tribes which inhabited Maranga and its surroundings were extremely bloodthirsty, if we judge by the human femurs sharpened to a point at one end, found by Jijon y Caamano in the third pyramid of Maranga alongside a trophy head and dismembered corpses. One cannot help wondering if these were used as weapons, insignia of victory, or daggers for sacrificing prisoners of war. Jijon y Caamano maintains that the ancient inhabitants of the district around Lima belonged to an 'aristocracy of conquerors' subject to powerful authority, of Andes origin but showing a strong Aymara influence. He offers proof of this in his discovery of a reed gondola over sixteen feet in length in the foundations of one of the *wakas*, identical in construction and appearance to those used even today by the fisher-folk of Lake Titicaca, on the Aymara plateau.

★   ★   ★

Wherever the famous oracle of Rimac may have spoken, it presents us with yet another mystery: did it give its name to the river, the valley, and the town of the ancient Wallas? Or did it originally have a different name, of Aymara origin, for Rimac is Quechua? If so, was Rimac 'imported' by the Incas, just as they imported the name Pachacamac, which is the Inca version of the ancient god Irma.

It is quite possible that Lima itself is merely a version of Irma, although this view is not commonly held. Even today the names Lima, Irma, or Rimac can sound remarkably similar when mumbled by contemporary Peruvians.

This, however, does not solve the problem of the oracle's origin.

Was it perhaps brought by the Wallas as they fled from the brutalities of Mama Wako and Manko? Or by the Walla servants of the Inca Huayna Kapak?

This is quite possible. For a very long time there has been a spot at Cuzco known as *Rimac-Pampa*, the 'talking place', very near the place where the Wallas were routed and where the Incas made their royal proclamations for their new territory.

Among the great architects of the Cyclopean fortress of Sacsahuaman, which dominates and protects Cuzco, we find recorded a certain Walla prisoner named Apu Walla Rimachi, condemned to forced labour. Inevitably to name Rimachi has attracted attention, and it has been maintained that all the derivatives of the word *rimac* (to speak) indicate a certain manner of speaking: either speaking a great deal, very quickly, volubly, loquaciously, criticising, declaiming, exaggerating, or talking in a vulgar way.

A picturesque rivalry was incurred between the talking gods of Rimac and Pachacamac. Wishing to distribute fairly the honours due to the two divinities, the Incas laid down that Pachacamac should be consulted on the affairs of royalty and the nobility, while the affairs of the common people should be dealt with at Rimac. At first this decision would seem to favour Pachacamac, but it had the reverse effect, as the common people were far more numerous, and the reputation of the oracle prospered accordingly throughout a very wide area. It may well be concluded that it was in fact the reputation of the oracle which gave the name Rimac to the valley and entire district.

An ancient document tells how the Indians of Lima laughed when they heard the Spaniards explain the name of the valley as being due to the gushing sound made by the river. The Spaniards clearly knew that *rimac* meant to speak, but knew nothing of the oracle, which at that time was consulted daily, and was venerated throughout the kingdom.

A century ago the *Waka* Juliana was still quite high. It was described in the 'nineties as a gaunt and sinister-looking hill rising from the sands, the frequent haunt of ghostly apparitions, unvisited by humanity, apart from the occasional planter who passed by on the way to his crops.

How different it is today! It is greatly reduced in height, surrounded by luxurious villas and colourful gardens, a mere stone's throw from one of the main streets of Lima.

Tales are told of an army of spectre horsemen who gallop up to the *waka* by night, carrying lighted torches and followed by great birds of prey. They vanish before sunrise, but at dawn the passer-by finds the soil churned up by hooves. Are these the ghosts of Pizarro and his *conquistadores*, or are they Bolivar's or San Martin's liberators?

Sometimes, we are told, the horsemen move aside to allow a white-robed girl to approach the *waka*. She seems to be searching for something, and disappears suddenly into the *waka*. This story has been interpreted as implying a search for buried treasure, and the *waka* bears witness to countless depredations throughout the centuries.

More recently, small boys of the locality have amused themselves by digging up mummies under cover of darkness, and perching them on top of the *waka* to welcome the neighbours next morning.

When Lima was building the endless Avenue Arquipa which runs to the sea, one of the workmen discovered at the foot of the *Waka* Juliana an ancient concealed entrance which opened into an interior gallery.

Sadly abandoned and profaned the sacred *wakas* are now—four centuries after the arrival of Pizarro—the Sunday meeting-place of the people of Lima. Plundered from every side, the grandiose pyramid of the Wallas is no more nowadays than a shapeless hillock, covering none the less an enormous surface. There are still, however, many thousands of mummies and other treasures awaiting the more gentle pick of the archaeologist today.

XIII

THE PAGAN CULT OF THE *WAKAS*

From one mystery we pass on to another—the mystery of the *wakas*. If the chroniclers of the conquest were not interested enough in the pre-Columbian pyramids to identify their exact sites, still less did they show any apparent interest in the people. If they bothered to mention the *waka* cult at all, it was only in order to revile the pagan religion which it symbolised, to condemn human or animal sacrifices, and to recommend the destruction of idols.

Oddly enough, it has been established that the *waka* was not at first a man-made monument, but a phenomenon of nature. Originally it was any strange shape—a curiously formed stone, a human being with four or six fingers, a vegetable or an animal which diverged from the normal, anything in short which appeared strange or unusual. They called the great Cordillera of the snowy sierra a *waka*, and this runs the whole length of Peru as far as the Straits of Magellan. They gave the same name to certain high peaks which were distinctive in shape, as well as to certain mountain ridges.

All these exceptional things were deified by the Indian of the sierras—inded even today he regards them as divine, and fears them, for he imagines them to be filled with a sacred fluid which may be either beneficial or disastrous, but which he must worship and placate.

In the Andes the primitive cult of the *wakas* was supplanted by a sun cult under the Incas; one cannot help wondering whether the conquerors from Cuzco, on being confronted with the sacred monument of these peoples, did not apply the name *waka* to the tiered and truncated pyramids which were not so called before. At all events it is known that the Incas also worshipped the *wakas*, for a sacred command laid down: 'No man shall blaspheme against the Sun my father, the Moon my Mother, against the stars, . . . or the *wakas*.'

The word itself is probably connected with the verb *quecha waka*, which means 'to implore, to groan, to call, to invoke, to cry, to sing, to palpitate'. This diversity of meaning will not seem strange to those who have seen Indians worshipping in church and addressing their favourite saint either in thanks or in reproach in vehement and tearful tones.

In the same way the worship of the *wakas* seems inseperably linked to that of the Indians' totem-worshipping ancestors, in whose honour there were periodic ritual feasts. The *waka* was both a social and religious symbol for the agricultural peoples living in its shadow. On the coast the *wakas* were undoubtedly sacred monuments fulfilling the function of temples, and burial places. In every *waka* a painted or embroidered cloth, or some ceremonial object, has been found decorated with a design which recalls the original totems of the sect.

Judging by remnants of *wakas* found both within the city of Lima and on the outskirts, it seems clear that each clan or *ayllus* situated on the Pacific coast has from the earliest days built one main pyramid dedicated to a sacred ancestor, surrounded by several pyramids of lesser size (as is illustrated by the three *wakas*, hardly visible nowadays, which surround the Sugar Loaf *Waka*). These undoubtedly belonged to the Walla Marka group.

Some of these subsidiary *wakas* may well have been connected with the cult of the stars, which were supposed to regulate the seasons and harvests.

Did the Incas respect them in the same way as they respected the Pachacamac and Rimac idols? Did the Spanish *conquistadores* steal the *adobe* from the ancient *wakas* to build their palaces, as the poor of Lima do today to build their miserable shacks? Indeed, the quantity of *adobe* bricks laid out horizintally and vertically is quite astonishing. Max Uhle has calculated that more than a million tons of bricks were used in the construction of *Waka* Juliana.

The first destruction dates back to the anger of Huayna Kapak, who destroyed the *wakas* because they 'refused to answer' him. Huaman Poma, who confesses himself unable to list all the idols and *wakas* of Chinchaysuyo on the grounds that they were so numerous tells us that this great Inca, who reigned shortly before the arrival of the Spaniards, was worried about the future and decided to question the *wakas*. 'Not one of them would reply', he tells us. Displeased by this, Huayna Kapak ordered the massacre of the priests and the destruction of the 'dumb *wakas*'. Very few escaped. *Waka* Pariakaka then pronounced that it was too late, and there was no point in speaking, as very soon men called *Viracocha* would come and govern in the name of an all-powerful master. On hearing this prophecy Huayna Kapak went away 'very sad and down-hearted'.

Many of the *wakas* must also have been ground down by the approaching avalanche of Incas and transformed into those masses of sand which were described in all the literature of the conquest as 'artificial hills'. We hear about this in a passage from *Relacion Anonima*, attributed to the Jesuit Blas Calera:

> After certain cruel wars . . . an order was given that earth should be thrown on the sepulchres and that they should be blocked up like hills. . . .

Those that were not thus camouflaged at that particular period, undoubtedly became so when the news of the arrival of Pizarro's *Viracochas* from the north was received, because Blas Valera adds:

> Nevertheless some still remained . . . but when it was known throughout the kingdom that the Spaniards had arrived armed to steal, kill, defile the temples and oratories, and pillage the villages lusting after gold and silver, it was decided to cover and hide all the sepulchres, and the treasures which could not be hidden should be thrown into the sea or the lakes.

Huaman Poma tells us why the *conquistadores* found so few idols
on their coast, apart from those of the god Rimac and his rival
Pachacamac, which were respected and left in their place by the
Incas. He tells us that all the idols of the conquered nations were
taken to Cuzco as hostages! The Incas would compel a group of the
conquered people to carry their chief idol to Cuzco and to house it
among hundreds of others in a temple like the Pantheon in Rome.
All the captured idols retained their inscriptions and their altars,
but they were symbolically chained to indicate the subjection imposed upon their people.

*   *   *

What exactly was the part played by the *waka* in the religion of
the ancient Peruvians of the coast? According to the majority of the
chroniclers, there seems to be no doubt that they were rich sepulchres.
'The Indians called their sacred places *wakas*, which is a sad name,'
explains Cieza de Leon, who continues: 'Many have been opened
and great quantities of gold and silver were found in them when
the Spaniards conquered the kingdom.'

Father Villar Cordova suggests that the inhabitants of the Peruvian
coast erected these pyramids of *adobe* because the desert stretches
provided them with no suitable raised ground for their temples,
accustomed as they were to worshipping the peaks of the Andes.
But he hesitates to class all *wakas* as temples. Some may have been
a form of watch-tower, to keep a watch on the surrounding country;
some may have been fortified mounds erected like castles to defend
or intimidate the peasant community. It seems as though the Incas
chose the most important *wakas* for fortifications while others were
quite simply outposts of the local *kuraka*. Some may have been
dwellings of priests, wizards, and servants of the princiapal *wakas*.

Middendorf, basing his ideas on ancient Egyptian customs,
considers that the *waka* may originally have been the personal
temple of the chief of the clan. On his death his successor would

build a new monument which would envelope and enlarge the
original one, it forming different levels both in height and width.
Each *waka* would thus become an expanding family tree of the tribe
or family whose ancestors had founded it.

Max Uhle goes further still in considering that the *waka* could
have been a sort of stadium, where ball games were played and where
the losers were sacrificed at the end of the match! It might even have
been an observatory in the tradition of the Incas of Cuzco, who set
great store by their astrologists; it would thus have been used to
indicate the days of the equinox calculated by the movement of the
shadows cast by the sun.

Some have even maintained that the *wakas* were the work of one
of the lost tribes of Israel because of their striking resemblance to the
tombs of some desert Hebrew tribes. Others again see in them the
copy of the Chaldaean ziggurats or the *teocallis* of Central America.

★   ★   ★

Whether the pre-Columbian *waka* of the Peruvian deserts was a
temple, a sanctuary, a fortification, an observatory, or a meeting-
place or stadium before becoming a necropolis, one thing is certain:
the monument had a mystic character which it preserved even after
the Spanish conquest, and in spite of the implacable ruthlessness
of the Franciscans, Dominicans, Augustinians, Jesuits, and other
missionaries of every sect sent to Peru to eradicate the widespread
paganism. This paganism had carved the myths of the desert people
on the fragile *adobe* in the form of exquisite frescoes—unfortunately
engraved on the very perishable stucco of the terraces. One could
contemplate incredible winged men, fish-men, crab-men, scorpion-
men, terrifying dragons, devil-cats, lunar goddesses on barks pulled
by shoals of fishes, two-headed snakes, not to mention a ballet of sea-
birds and a whole galaxy of stars round an anthropomorphic sun.
Of these frescoes practically nothing remains.

Along came an army of Spanish priests, armed with cross and

breviary, and rabid in their mission of rooting out the pagan creed of the Indians; the priests were accompanied by the *conquistadores* with cloak and dagger, eager to despoil the Indians of their riches.

One of the most ruthless, Pedro de Villagomez, the Archbishop of Lima tells how in the course of *A Visit to the Idolaters* it was remarked that the Indians who had become Christian still had their communal *wakas* in the centre of the village, and even private *wakas* belonging to each family, and that they held feasts in their honour, made sacrifices and brought offerings to them. These *wakas* were looked after by 'priests and officers of varying rank employed in the ministry of their idolatrous practices'. Many superstitions and ancestral traditions were still observed.

In many places the 'Indians removed the corpses from the churches and buried them in the fields, because their dead were happier in the open air rather than being suffocated in the churches'. This was undoubtedly an ingenuous lie, as one can imagine that the Indians wanted to rescue their dead and place them in the *waka* with the mummies of their ancestors, as tradition compelled them all to rest together in the *waka* which had been prepared to receive their dead. But even today the Indian knows instinctively how to disguise the truth when he is forced to reply to a stranger whom he considers incapable of understanding.

PLATE XIII

A *cochimilco*—little doll-shaped idol—made into à ceremonial container.

Magnificent ceremonial vase made of red and white clay, decorated with two raised serpents.

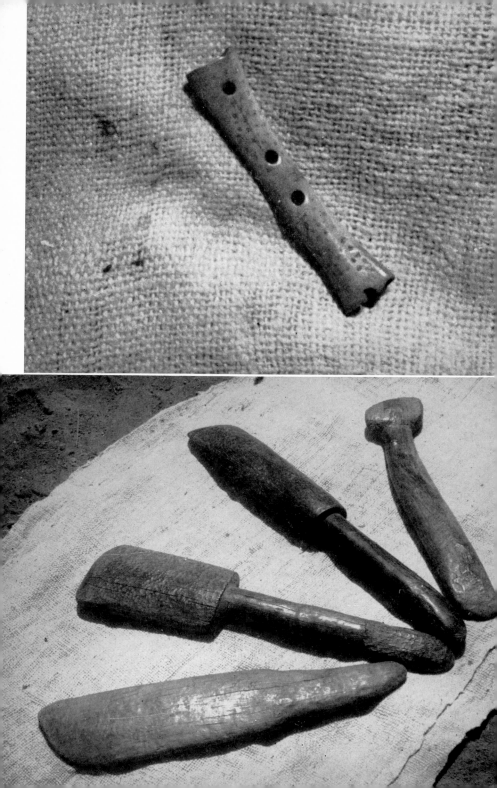

It may be that the extraordinary cult of the *wakas* described by the priests who were the chroniclers of the conquest were exaggerated accounts, mainly because of this lack of comprehension. However, the details furnished by the first great Indian or half-caste writers not only coincide in their descriptions, but add many astonishing details. Let us see how Archbishop Villagomez explains the cult of the *wakas* in a chapter devoted to the 'Exhortations and Instructions for the Idolatrous Indians'.

Numerous servants were necessary, and their jobs were so minutely defined that the 'priest of each *waka* was independent of the others', but he had special very strict obligations concerning a 'well-regulated ritual which nobody could change'. Here is a list given by him concerning the 'ministers of idolatry':

The *wakapvillak*, 'the one who speaks to the *waka*', was generally the oldest priest. He was the Guardian of the *waka*, he answered the people's questions, 'telling them only the things that they had to know', carried the offerings, made sacrifices, ordered the fasts, arranged for the provision of food on feast-days, recited legends, and initiated the ignorant into the practices of idolatory.

PLATE XIV

A llama-bone *quena* (flute), life-size, decorated with little carved circles. Note the remarkable regularity in the weave of the material on which it is lying, and in which its owner was wrapped.

Four pre-Columbian agricultural tools.

I

The *mallkivillak*, 'the one who speaks to the *mallkis*', a minor minister, an assistant, and the sacristan.

The *maksa* or *villak*, 'one who performs cures by means of superstitions and tricks—the cures are preceded by sacrifices in the manner of the *waka*'.

The *aukachic* was an assistant who took confessions during the feast of the *waka*, and on journeys.

The *asuak* (or *accak*) was in charge of the food for the feasts and offerings, and might be of either sex but was usually a man on the coast and a woman in the mountains.

The *sociak*—sometimes referred to as *wallak* (charm diviner)—read his prognostications from a mound of maize. If the number he saw there was an even number all was well, if not, woe betide!

The *rapiak* was another diviner, who answered questions from his consultants while feeling their biceps. If there was a reflex from the right arm it was a good sign, but if on the left side it was bad.

The *pacharikuk* or *pachakuk* foretold the future on examination of large furry spiders' legs. He kept these creatures in holes in the walls or under stones, and laid them on a blanket and beat them with a stick to break their legs. He made his predictions according to the number of broken legs.

The *moskok* interpreted dreams. He had to be given a piece of clothing to sleep with, hair or clothes if the problem was one to do with love—the cloak, the *chuspa* (*coca* bag) or the *waraka* (turban) for men, or the *chumbi* (belt) for women.

The *hakarikok* or *cuirikok*—This individual prognosticated by means of examining the entrails of guinea-pigs, according to the part which moved or the part from which blood flowed.

Nor is this all, for some of these 'priests' or 'ministers' of the *wakas* are even more sinister in practice, for example the *runapmikuk* or *kauchu*, 'those who eat man', and especially children. The Archbishop further alleges that they sprinkled the powdered bones of the dead, muttering spells in order to put people to sleep, so that they could enter their houses undisturbed. They would then scratch victims, suck their blood from the wound and spit it into the palm of their hand to 'increase their magic powers'. Alternatively they would take away the blood in a small receptacle and mix it with their meat at meals, thus bringing about the death of the victim a few days later.

The Walla sorcerers sacrificed llamas and guinea-pigs to the *wakas*, and spat out the sacrificial blood in order to make the oracle of the *waka* speak.

What form did these sacrifices take? The priests were in a state of ecstasy produced by a narcotic called *tonka*, made from the fruit of a date palm. They would tear out the heart of the llama and eat it, pouring the blood on the *waka*. There were also human sacrifices, but children were only sacrificed to the principal *waka* of each zone. The sacrificial blood was sometimes used to anoint the face of the idol, as well as the face of the victim.

Archbishop Villagomez also tells us how a *waka* priest was appointed. The first way was by succession, the son inheriting the office from his father. If the son had not reached the age of discretion the next of kin undertook the office during the interim. Secondly, if there was no heir the successor was chosen by election, preference being shown to those who had been struck by lightning, to lunatics, or to those suffering from heart disease. Thirdly, anyone could volunteer for the job, but one can imagine that the rigorous fasts and penitence to which both male and female priests had to submit would not make for willing volunteers. Those who volunteered to serve the *waka* had to undergo a period of several months without spices, women, washing themselves, combing or brushing their hair, or touching their body with their hands. The Archbishop concludes that it was generally old men or women who volunteered to be priests, and that they only did so as a means of subsistence. After the severe initiation period they lived on the offerings and the meat of the sacrifices, so they may have done quite well for themselves in the long run.

We find that the principal *waka* was fêted solemnly three or four times a year and that the Indians devoutly hold that these feasts were instituted by the *wakas* themselves.

The *Runanakak*—'the one who makes people suffer'—supervised the preparation of the great public confession. Consulting the *waka*, he would announce that it desired to be fêted on a certain day. He would then issue his orders. One man was put in charge of fetching water, another wood, another shellfish, llamas, and pigs, while the women and children ground the maize from the *waka's* sacred field, whose yield was reserved for the use of the priests and mummies.

Boiling fermented maize produced a creamy if bitter drink unexpectedly inebriating, especially as it was often accompanied by stimulants. In the valley of Chancay next to Lima, *espingo* powder was added. The *espingo* is a small dry fruit, almond-shaped and of very unpleasant smell. This drink is peculiar to Peru, and was circulated in gourds and jugs. This ritual drinking made people servants of the gods.

Other worshippers, whose bodies were painted in stripes, would display coloured incense and paint powders used in the *waka*.

The servants of the *waka* were still extremely numerous at the beginning of the Spanish occupation. Archbishop Villagomez tells us that many of the children who were destined for the service of the *wakas* were brought up in hiding so that they could neither be baptised nor recorded in the parish register.

A dozen days of fast, similar to the customary fast of the *waka* priests, preceded the feast. It was forbidden for men and women to sleep together during this period. This period was accompanied by the famous confessions to which all had to submit, and present themselves washed and dressed in new clothes of the brightest colours.

On arrival at confession, the Indian had to incite the ritual phrase: 'Encircling mountains, valleys, flying vultures and owls listen, for I am about to confess my sins.' He pronounced these words with his right hand raised, holding in his fingers the *mullu*—a piece of shell threaded on to a long thorn. Seated in a circle around the confessor, the other penitents listened, accusing him at times of thefts, of treating others badly, of adultery, and even of paying reverence to the God of the Spaniards.

His sins confessed, the penitent would hand the *mullu* to the confessor, who stuck the thorn into his cloak, forcing it until it broke. If the thorn broke in three pieces, the confession had been honest. If not, the penitent was obliged to begin again, and this time must hide or omit nothing.

The confessional rite varied, according to the clan. It was also carried out with a dried stick of *ichu* or with guinea-pig's blood. The penitent would have his hands fastened behind his back, and was beaten with a stick.

Each penitent handed the *runanakak* the offering powder, which he placed on the *pasca* (the flat pardoning stone). The powder was mixed with white maize flour and rubbed on the penitent's forehead. The confessional rite ended in a purifying bath at the juncture of two rivers or canals.

The *Pacarikuk*, or eve of the feast, was celebrated by dancing, singing, and listening to stories. This continued throughout the night.

Great demonstrations of joy greeted the dawn. The priests met on the highest platform of the *waka*, magnificently dressed in finely embroidered white tunics under a headdress of multicoloured feathers. If the totem of the *waka* was an animal, the costumes and masks all symbolised this 'ancient inhabitant'.

The crowd bit their nails or pulled out their eyelashes to blow them towards the summit of the *waka*, where only the priests were permitted to stand. The offerings consisted in little mascots made from maize paste moistened with blood.

Some of the sacred *chicha* was then poured generously on to the terraces of the *waka*—at this stage the liquid was very thick and of high alcoholic content. The rest was offered to the priests, who lost no time in becoming extremely drunk.

One of them finally intoned the invocation to the *waka*, calling it *runapkamak* (raiser of men) offering it beautiful and rich presents: 'Lord,' he prayed adding the name of the divinity of the clan, then making a kissing sound with his lips, 'I have come bringing you these things offered by your children. Receive them and be not enraged. Give them long lives, health and good harvests.'

Then the blood from the sacrificial animals or children was added to the *chicha* now flowing down from the pyramid; the favourite sacrifices were flawless white llamas, guinea-pigs, and probably new-born children—preferably twins. Happy was the man or woman who had the good fortune to be splashed with this blood.

The priests took the hearts from the victims to offer them to the god, and the god spoke to them. It is believed that portents were read from the pulsating entrails, and the waiting people would be all agog to hear the news.

These sacrifices were accompanied by singing and music from shell trumpets (the *pututus*) or horns made from leather or silver. It sometimes happened that the idol was displayed in a procession on the sea-front.

Naturally the orgies of *chicha* which accompanied the feasts did not pass uncriticised by the prudish Villagomez. This we can understand even better when we learn that the priests encouraged homosexuality and even organised 'public houses' where the homosexuals could be distinguished by their clothes.

There were many good priests and magicians eager that the *wakas* should be worshipped in a fitting manner, but there were also many 'false magicians' who made a living by exploiting the people, and claiming power to cure all manner of illnesses by means of consultation with demons.

★   ★   ★

One can understand how these superstitious practices and magic rites filled the religious Spaniards with indignation; had they not

come to convert the Peruvians? But this indignation was recipro-
cated by the local priests, who could not accept the one God of the
Christians, nor the Virgin and saints who were content with holy
water!

Thus it was that the priests met secretly in order to institute the
'Commandments of the *wakas*', drawn up as a counterblast to the
order which Villagomez had decreed to wipe out idolatry.

Here is a strange summary:

1. The Indians were forbidden to recognise other gods besides those
   of their *wakas*. Disobedience meant immediate death and
   penalties would be imposed on their descendants for the next
   four generations.

2. Annual feasts should always be celebrated with spotless white
   animals (though the colour of guinea-pigs, was held to be of no
   importance).

3. Indians and children offered to the *wakas* must not be baptised,
   and must have no imperfection or any mole on their bodies.

4. No spiders, toads, frogs, nor snakes should be killed at normal
   times but should be kept for sacrifice.

5. Confession must take place each year. Absolution would be
   granted ritually by placing a wire or thread on the head of the
   penitent, while intoning sacred phrases. This was to be followed
   by a ritual cleansing in spring water.

6. No salt or spices were to be taken during the period of abstinence
   which preceded these festivals—nor was there to be any sexual
   intercourse.

7. The Indians must be properly dressed to kiss the *waka*, while
   pulling out their eyelashes and eyebrows.

8. They must continue to bury their dead in the ancient sepulchres,
   making them the same sacrifices as were made to the *wakas*.

9. They must change their clothes every year and give them food
   and water on the ceremonial day of the dead.

10. Wherever a Christian priest or missionary had been seen, a black dog must be walked to and fro. The dog should then be thrown into the river to drown, thus absorbing the Christian influence and purifying the ground.

11. No dealings were to be had with Christian priests or missionaries, enemies of the *wakas*.

12. White stones, or even blades of straw, should be offered to the *waka* when crossing or walking on its road.

13. Casual visitors or passers-by must be encouraged to venerate their own personal *wakas*.

14. None of these commandments was to be revealed to the Spaniards, on pain of slow starvation, plague, and death.

XIV

WALLALLO, GOD OF FIRE AND BLOOD

One of the strange rites of the *wakas* leads us for the last time, with the Wallas, along the steep mountain path carved on the sides of the valley of Rimac, to the cyclopean temple of the great god Wallallo.

It may well be that the idol carved in the rock was the god of the Wallas of Lima, who left the mark of their cult on the narrow canyon of Rimac before the arrival of the Huanchos, who came from the high plateaux and installed themselves there with their god *Pariakaka*—the dangerous and cunning rival of Wallallo, whose equestrian battles we shall later enlarge upon.

The legendary story unfolds in the outskirts of the little Andean village of Casta, where in 1923 Tello saw a young white llama being sacrificed in secret to the glory god of the Wallas, to whom the Yachik priests brought offerings of guinea-pig blood, *coca* leaves, and *chicha*.

At this recent date—and possibly even today—Wallallo continued to be, for the superstitious Indians of this valley, 'the one who commanded the rains, the springs, the rivers, and all sources of water'. This means a very important deity indeed, when one realises that the fantastic drama of the Andean sky may engulf entire villages under tons of snow and mud and stones, or alternatively and more frequently, leave them quite without water for years, causing the disappearance of livestock, famine, and death.

Tello describes in some detail the fantastic invocations to Wallallo during the festival celebrated on the first Sunday of October to urge the god to give them abundant water and to fill their canals and reservoirs and *acequias*, many of which had been inherited from pre-Columbian times. One of these reservoirs was the Walla-Cocha, fed by the snow from the peak of this name, and the great glacier Kalla Walla.

The people of Casta told Tello that at the beginning of the Indian year—in June, when the Pleiades appeared—the inhabitants used to leave their dwellings and walk in a great procession towards one of the most famous *wakas*, the *waka* of Wallallo, where the dreadful spectacle of human sacrifice was demanded annually by the god.

All the *ayllus* of the mountain were invited to this *waka*, and each came with the idol and the magnificently dressed ancestral mummies of the clan at the head of a motley retinue, dressed in brilliant new clothes.

The female sacrifice was chosen from a different *ayllu* each year. She must be the most beautiful virgin, of absolute purity, without the slightest physical defect, blemish, nor any illness. Tello conjures up the spectacle for us.

Now we see her advancing, her multicoloured cloak of exquisite embroidery covered with flowers. She walks slowly, regally, possibly drugged. Beside her clamber the priests and magicians, at the head of a long winding procession, higher and higher up the steep track. The crowd are singing and dancing, playing their pipes and beating rhythmically on their drums. The ritual demands that all should be gay to comfort the destined victim. Along the path are strewn the petals of beautiful flowers, their delicate exotic perfume being a gift to the god of these frozen altitudes. If we lift our eyes we may contemplate one of the highest peaks of the Andes. At around 13,000 feet, a fortress may be discerned, having five colossal walls (similar to the three parapets of Sacsahuaman above Cuzco) built in the form of a pyramid. This pyramid ends in a narrow platform where up to two hundred little rooms can be counted.

To reach this fortress we must follow a path which zig-zags with a very sharp gradient, and is beautifully maintained; when we reach the fourth upward coil of the path there are two monolithic, trapezoidal gates, each opening on to a stairway cut sharply into the granite, and almost vertical.

Higher still, the two stairways join to make one single flight of even steeper steps. Even looking at them from below we feel dizzy, and this sensation increases as we climb higher and higher. Panting with the crowd, we reach the rocky height at last. Hardly have we arrived than the magicians stop us, inviting the older members of each clan to follow them and be allotted a place. Places are disposed according to age and social position, in order to worship the idols.

The sacrifice approaches. The flute-players, drum-beaters, and singers follow the young victim to the temple of Wallallo, where a great gulf yawns in the mountainside.

One last time, as though hesitant, the young virgin stops and listens to the screaming crowd. But already the magicians have announced the offering of flesh and blood to the god, whose hunger will be satisfied by the perfect sacrifice, and who will then answer the plea of his subjects to send rain and good harvests.

The victim is led to the edge of the gulf, and we see her throw herself down.

*   *   *

In the early days after the Spanish conquest the idol Wallallo was found, quite by chance, by some Augustinian fathers in the Cordillera. There they saw the Indians daubing the god of rock with the blood of slaughtered guinea-pigs, and offering piles of bones and horns, together with a heap of wooden weapons.

This idol was destroyed by the first *corregidor* of Huarochiri, Diego Davila Briceno, at the time of the suppression of the Indians decreed by the viceroy of Peru. Briceno left us some observations on this subject:

The Indians of this province recount that the Yungas of the valley of
Lima arrived there after the wars and peopled the foot of the high
snow covered sierras of Pariakaka, where they kept their idol Wallallo,
to whom they sacrificed women and children.

These are interesting details, as they support the opinion we have
already put forward as to the itinerary of the Wallas and the pre-
Inca population of Lima.

Tello describes their descendants four hundred years later. These
people had forgotten nothing of the ancient tradition, despite the
continuous efforts of the Catholic Church, though the ritual had
softened a little and the sacrificial victims no longer included humans.
The priest-magician still climbed the sacred peak—but in secret,
under cover of darkness, so as not to be seen by the police or missionaries who have forbidden pagan ceremonies—carrying in a little
red bag leaves of *coca*, powdered tobacco mixed with *chamico*, a jar
of *chicha* and a phial of strong vitriolic alcohol made from sugar
cane. Now, however, he was accompanied by only four people.
Once at the summit the ancient ritual phrases were repeated. Did
Wallallo always reply?

Tello describes the magician in the moonlight, his ear pinned to
the mountain. The expression on his face indicates to his four
companions that the voice of the idol has spoken to him. As though
hypnotised, they advance at his command and lay down their
offerings. This ritual act completed, the great magician goes into
the ruined temple alone to the presence of a grimacing mummy.

The magician talks with this impressive personage, whose wrinkled
skin he anoints with the blood of a sacrificed guinea-pig, and then,
drunk with alcohol and excitement, goes out to tell his companions
what the mummy has replied.

All night long the five men play their melancholy dirges on reed
flutes—instruments which convey admirably the solitude of the
Indian living in the Andes; the colourful days of the past gone for
ever, and he is oppressed by the thousand misfortunes of modern

times. These dirges continue until the last star has been consumed by the dawn.

Guided by the magician, the five men make their perilous descent down the side of the abyss, while the first rays of golden sun—the only gold which the Indians ever see now—melts the veils of the enshrouding mist.

In the valley below, the village people await them anxiously, to hear the oracular pronouncements of the mummy of Wallallo. Several days of orgys and feasting follow, and finally there is the rite of worshipping the canals which have been there for time immemorial.

The water is temporarily rechannelled, and each *acequia* (flagged in stone by the pre-Columbians) is solemnly cleaned with infinite care. Whenever the precious water is allowed to flow back, the men immerse themselves up to the waist, fully dressed and holding hands. This curious icy baptism is accompanied by the *Song of the Waters*— the great hymn to Wallallo which is sung in choir by all the assembled clans:

> At last Walla-Walla is with you!
> Now, indeed all will be well . . .
> > Walla, Walla
> Water descending in three streams
> Come to gladden our soil
> > Walla, Walla
> Gushing fount
> Come feed our pastures,
> > Walla, Walla . . . *etc.*

It is still unknown, however, who this powerful and legendary Wallallo was, who has been worshipped in such great pomp from long before the days of the Incas—up to the present day. He is mentioned in numerous accounts as one of the most important of the great divinities of the Andean pantheon, and we see him century after century, together with many other gods of ancient Peru, ruling the life—and particularly the agricultural life—of the people.

According to tradition, the original Indians were children of the great mountain peaks, and these became symbols of the vanished people who were the creators of Peruvian civilisation. Among them was Wallallo.

Here we find ourselves once again in the phantasmagorical world of the gods of the Andean Cordillera.

Viracocha-Sun, one myth tells us, laid five eggs on the summits of Condor Koto, which loomed over the Sierra of Lima. From these eggs four muses were hatched: Pariakaka, Clear-Water, Wampu (the great and cunning rival of Wallallo), and Clear-Fire (who was endowed with a curious gift of fecundity, for he could implant twins in the wombs of humans, animals, plants, and even inanimate objects!).

Thus it was that while travelling through the Cordillera we saw an Indian woman burying a double-yoked egg which she regarded as magic, and which she hoped would bring an equally magic harvest to the field where she put it.

Tello maintains that the mythological world of the Indian is a faithful reflection of his own world and illustrates this by the myth of Wallallo. Even today the Indians of the cordilleras pronounce the name of Wallallo only on certain occasions always connected with unusual weather conditions. We may thus consider Wallallo as the supreme master of the forces of nature.

When Wallallo is described to us as a monster who reappears temporarily at the beginning of the rainy season, running in all directions over the mountain tops and the *quebradas*, his eyes flashing fire which illuminates the horizon, roaring like a wild beast and releasing the rain, there is no need to be very imaginative to see Wallallo personified in the storm which renders the earth fruitful by producing rain.

The Indian will tell us that Wallallo has just come back from Kollao. This return is anxiously awaited each year, as all crops depend on these electric storms, descending as they do in terrifying force on the 'roof' of South America.

The Indian lives almost as an acrobat, cultivating a tiny plot of land suspended on the side of the mountain; herdsman of a few llamas which provide him with wool for his clothes, meat for his pot, thongs for his catapult, leather for his shoes, bones for his flutes, and fat for his rituals. His mode of life has indeed hardly changed one iota during the last millennium. When we have seen this Indian's life blasted and his property destroyed by a storm the like of which exists nowhere else in the world, the legend of Wallallo becomes as clear to us as the sacred water which is the object of his deepest desires.

As the legend depicts Wallallo causing great harm to the Indians who disobey him, killing men and livestock, we understand the reason for the obligatory sacrifices: should one not try to appease the awful god by offering him his favourite drink—human blood? It is this blood which is destined to renew and conserve life, the magic blood transfusion which kept their ancestors eternally young.

Another legend would have us believe that Wallallo was a cannibal, by describing how he ordered a woman whom he has just created to give birth to twins, one of which he would devour! It may be in this apparent cannibalism that we should look for the main reason for the terrific battles which were said to take place between Wallallo and his powerful rivals Pariakaka and Wampu. There were other local deities—and peaks of the Andes—to whom the Indian tradition attributes innumerable marvellous feats.

All these deities assume the shape of a man from time to time. A story is told of an Indian who, undertaking a ritual pilgrimage to Wallallo, went laden with offerings to the god. Among these gifts was his own son, whom he intended offering as food. On the way he met Pariakaka, who asked the Indian where he was going. He tried to persuade the Indian to substitute a llama for his son as a victim, but the trembling Indian refused, for, he explained, 'Wallallo will kill us all in his fury!' Seeing that the other god was irritated by his explanation, he added: 'He makes it rain yellow and red. The lighting appears in five different places at once, and after five days of terrible hailstorms, whole villages are swept into the sea, so that not one of the inhabitants escapes his wrath.'

(The people of Huarochiri showed us the visible traces of one of these monstrous cataclysms, which had swept the village of Huaquinusa into the sea.)

The legend concludes that Pariakaka then understood the great hold Wallallo had over the Indian population, and realising that he could not be dissuaded from his horrible diet, he promised to wage war on the cruel god, and banish him for ever.

The chronicler Francisco de Avila tells us that Wallallo and Pariakaka fought for three days and nights. Pariakaka hurled a great quantity of water and hail on Wallallo, who was unable to withstand the assault and was cast down from the steep slopes of the Andes. Until this day there exists a lake called Pariakaka into which all the water fell, on the Royal Way which leads to Cuzco. It is said that the two protagonists were transformed into mountains after this battle, which is probably the legendary version of a cataclysmic volcanic eruption.

From that time on the power of the Walla god constantly diminished, and we hear a curious tale of amorous rivalries which mingled with the increasing horror of human sacrifices to reduce his authority.

Expelled from the Cordillera of Yauyos by Pariakaka, he was later worshipped in the region of Casta to the north. But his rivals did not allow him to enjoy this prestige for long, for Pariakaka organised all the gods of the district in league against him. How did they set about the conquest of the Walla hero? Quite simply by using a little low cunning, and the attractions of sex!

One of these gods, Wampu, who was particularly covetous of the forests and pastures which enriched Wallallo's domain, was determined to remove his opponent. For this purpose he spent a long time in preparation, drinking human blood provided by his people in order to strengthen himself for the assault. Then he set several traps, but Wallallo outwitted him cunningly.

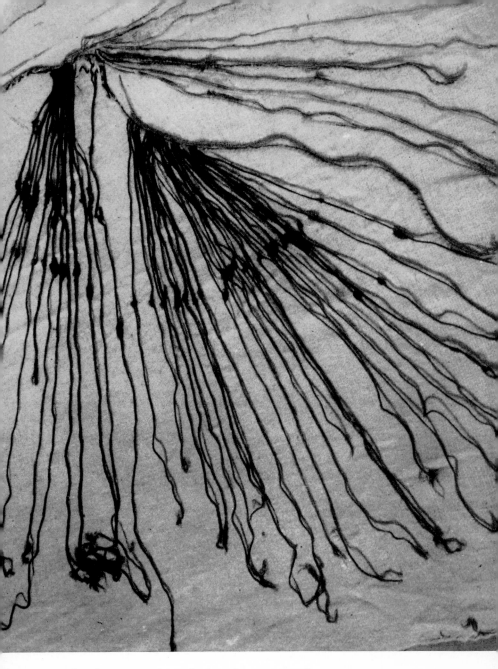

A very fine *kipu* turned up during the course of excavations on the pre-Inca palace of Puruchucu in the Rimac valley, about eight miles from Lima, at the foot of the Andes.

PLATE XV

Our astounding Walla High Priestess is without any doubt the proud possessor of the longest hair in the world: more than seven feet long!

Judging by the state of her teeth, she cannot have been more than twenty-five years old.

PLATE XVI

Knowing that the enterprising Wallallo favoured several goddesses with his attention, offering them the stars as their reward, and aware that there was one goddess whom he found particularly attractive, Wampu asked her to allow herself to be seduced by Wallallo. Then at the very moment when Wallallo thought he had obtained his desire she tore off one of his testicles,[1] at the same time calling Wampu and the other gods to her aid.

At this signal the clamour of the rival gods and goddesses was so terrific, the thunder so overwhelming, the flashes of lightning so dazzling and the rain so appalling that, in his hurry to escape the onslaught, Wallallo did not immediately realise that he had been robbed of one of his most precious attributes—the very one with which he procreated twins and fertilised the Indian lands, producing abundant crops of maize, potatoes, *quinoa* (corn), *coca*, and flowers.

Wampu hid Wallallo's testicle in a grotto, where a magician from Lake Titicaca was taking shelter from the cold while crossing the Cordillera. He had been collecting herbs and looking for magic stones or insects which might be useful to him in his calling of magician-healer. The man realised the importance of the find immediately, for would it not enable him to perform miracles which only the gods could perform? He set out with his treasure for the high plateaux of Kollao, but died on the journey. Wampu and his people recovered the testicle and this time they hid it where it was safe from marauding magicians.

It is supposed that Wampu, mythical hero and chief rival of Wallallo, was also a Walla by origin, who was jealous of the sexual prowess of his master. The names Wampu and Wallallo still survive as the peaks on which their contest was fought.

The disappearance of Wallallo, the legend concludes, meant the ruin of all his people. The lands became barren, the forests which provided the wood to build houses and temples, as well as for cooking, the vast pasture lands of llamas and alpaca, all disappeared

---

[1] 'Wallallo' is said to mean testicle in Quecha. We know that the virile parts are the totem for certain Indian tribes, for instance the Antix of Huaylas.

K

and became Wampu's domain. Several years passed in terrible drought which in its turn caused innumerable plagues. All these misfortunes decimated Wallallo's people. Some time later he re-appears under the name of Wallallo-Carhuancho, in the form of the fertilising rain. But these annual visits did not continue for long, and his people took to building dams to collect the precious water.

It is said that at this time Wallallo joined the Chankas and Huankas in their vain struggle against the Incas, who condemned both him and Pariakaka to work on the building of the fortress of Sacsahuaman and the Sun Temple of Pachacamac.

*   *   *

A great deal of useful information may be culled from this legend. We note the essentially agrarian character of the Walla civilisation, in which all activities have a single aim—the fertility of the soil, intelligent irrigation of the soil, the coaxing of the crops in one of the most physically hostile zones of the Cordilleras.

Even today we find bordering the track a great many peaks and lakes which bear the name of ancient deities—the way having been trodden by the countless feet of their worshippers on the way to offer some bloody gift. One particularly interesting track—steep and twisting—leads to the well-encircled temple of Wampu from the ancient 'dead' city of Cajamarquilla, a few miles from Lima. Here it is lost in a labyrinth of sandy streets in this ruined city.

When Pariakaka decided to suppress the human sacrifices, the legend gives us a historical lesson, showing us the great chief exhorting his men to abandon the bloodthirsty hero. Storms occur with ferocious power in the Andes, and have an enormous effect on the lives of the people.

The historian Tschudi, in a handwritten manuscipt, deduces 'that the Fire God' and the 'Rain God' were two rival chiefs whose tribes waged war against each other while the Yungus travelled along the coast, and on their travels founded a little village named Lima.

XV

THE PERUVIAN DEITIES OF THE PACIFIC

The intense greed for gold and silver, which was the mainspring of the Spaniards' arrival in the first place, meant that very little was discovered during the early years after the conquest about the ancient customs and the 'false' Peruvian religion. The Jesuit Blas Valera, writing some time after the conquest, regrets this lack of interest. It is in this fantastic pantheon, which flourished all along the Pacific coast of Peru, that we find the foundation of the religious beliefs of those ancient peoples.

This equatorial area is one of quite exceptional climatic conditions, and there is no doubt that these conditions have stamped their imprint on the religious beliefs of the people. A mysterious cold current sweeps the coast (the Humboldt Stream). Tempests of incredible violence—starting and stopping with dramatic suddenness —lash down on the settlements on the Andes road near Lima. It is no wonder that these people have always been markedly conscious of terrestrial, maritime, and celestial phenomena.

At the base of these theogonic religions, which sprang from a desire to interpret—or rather to justify—the most extraordinary climate, the Yungas placed an idolatry of monuments, where spiritualism, totemism, fetishism, magic liturgy, would be fused together in fantastic rituals celebrated on or around the *wakas*, which were probably built by the first inhabitants of the coast about 2,000 years ago—possibly even more, but this is the age generally agreed upon for these layered pyramids similar to those of Pachacamac to the south of Lima.

With the building of the *wakas*, the religion of the ancient idolatries became gradually more organised and took on a definite form based on the changing seasons, the sowing of the grain, and the harvests. Thus it was that, thanks to collective organisation and despite the aridity of the soil, the lack of cattle, tools, and means of transport, an archaic agriculture developed into a means of supporting a population of several million people, not to mention their numerous gods and mummies.

Cowed by the powerful natural elements, impressed by the immense expanses of sea and land, the inhabitant of the coast found a mental escape in a mythology swarming with gods and demons in the forms of animals, men, and plants which are represented on the pottery, the cloth, the ornaments, and the walls of the city, but which, hitherto, have hardly been studied.

*   *   *

Every island off the Peruvian coast was at one time the scene of events of unimaginable horror. Traces of this horror are still to be found recorded in stark realism on the relics of thousands of years ago. These bare, rocky islets, which are now haunted only by the sad cries of the *guaneros* (sea-birds), were named after gods. When the thick layers of guano which covered the isles at the time of the conquest were penetrated, altars were found at the foot of which lay mummies of decapitated young women.

It is curious to note that because of their aridity, which made them uninhabitable by man, these black islands, painted white and yellow by the excrement of the birds, were considered in the mythology as gods in disgrace.

The guano of these sea-birds enriched the arid soil to some extent, so it is perhaps no surprise that the bird was deified and that we saw it exquisitely depicted on a finely woven cloth found on a mummy of Puruchuchu. This cloth was actually discoloured and stained in places by guano, which seems to prove that the Huanchos of Puruchuchu used this natural manure, living as they did at the foot of the Andes more than ten miles from the sea. The Bird God is represented floating on swirling waves which seethe with all the typical marine life of the Humboldt Stream. It is placed in the centre of the cloth under the outline of a very elegant crested heron, wearing on its shoulder a ceremonial paddle or ritual sceptre. Mounted on a skiff drawn by a shoal of fish, this Bird God is very probably Waman Kantax, whom the natives went to worship on the island of Mazorka, which lay opposite the port of Huacho, to the north of Lima. Here they built a *waka*.

★   ★   ★

We are told that before the people embarked for this island, ritual demanded a two-day fast, during which the beach was sprinkled with *chicha*, so that neither strong winds nor rocks should harm the convoy of dainty reed-rafts. When the people reached the rocky island, they probably offered *chicha* and sacrificed virgins to Waman Kantax, to persuade him to permit them to peel off layers of the marvellous if evil-smelling guano.

What frightful scenes must have occurred on this island, and others like it! The *wakas* themselves provide some evidence, and in some of the chronicles we read of rich young beauties decked in turquoises, their breasts covered with gold and silver, their heads severed on board the rafts—the blood mingling with the salt water, or possibly lying decapitated or with their throats cut at the foot of the idol.

The echo of these events and their riches, hidden under many feet of guano, came to the ears of the fisher-pirates at the end of the last century. They invaded this fantastic cluster of rocks, which varied from a hundred to four hundred feet high, jutting out of the Pacific like vestiges of a mountain range swallowed up countless millennia ago. Undoubtedly these men were not expecting the overpowering smell of ammonia given off by the guano, the Peruvian 'white gold' which, on certain islands, could be found over 160 feet thick, and which they had to attack with picks in order to extract the covered idols, destroying millions of *guaneros* in the process—birds which the ancient peoples had always protected. It was Humboldt who sent a few ounces of this guano to Europe to be analysed, and to him we owe the knowledge of this marvellous fertiliser which is richer than any other natural or chemical manure, and which was the basic wealth of the desert Peruvians.

In the southern islands, opposite Chincha, mummies were discovered splendidly dressed in the famous embroidered blankets of Paracas, wearing little bags of guano round their necks. Could it be to fertilise the unknown lands beyond?

Villagomez, Archbishop of Lima, gives us a vivid picture of the guano ritual in a pastoral letter which he wrote in 1649. He tells us that after two days of fast the rafts returned laden with guano, which they unloaded on to the beaches to the accompaniment of gay songs and dances.

Villagomez goes on to describe a ritual which was still current in the seventeenth century, judging it to be 'a most prejudicial abuse': in December, he recounts, after five days of abstinence when the avocado pears in the valleys were beginning to ripen, they had a feast called *Akatay Mita* which lasted for six days and nights. Men and women met naked on a little esplanade between the plots, where a race was arranged over a considerable distance, the women being given a start. It was understood that the men had free right to any women they caught during the race—and there were no inhibitions.

Von Tschudi, who knows Quecha well, translates *Akatay Mita* as meaning 'the time of rapid coition'. He demonstrates that this was undoubtedly a feast with a deep religious significance. 'Its aim,' he supposes, 'was not simply a sexual debauchery.' The *Akatay Mita* was probably carried out in the presence of the priests, although the ritual imbibing of *chicha* undoubtedly added to the effect. It was, therefore, a kind of obligatory ritual service—a duty to accomplish in order to ensure the ripening of the fruit.

The *Akatay Mita* seems to have been a very old custom of the

Mochica-Chimu, which figures on the illustrations of the ceremonial *wakas*. There are some immense paintings of mountain peaks
and ravines, bays and islands, on which sea-wolves, fish, and *guaneros*
play, as well as scenes of sacrifices presided over by fantastic beings
—wizards and witches dressed as land or sea-going demons and
animals in human form. Dr. Rebecca Carrion-Cachot quotes
instances of couples in sexual copulation, which she claims support
the account of Villagomez. Tello tells us that the *Akatay Mita* was
a ritual of the 'return of the guano' the human coupling symbolising
the fertile power with which the guano endows the soil.

The fertility of the soil and of humans is a real obsession with the
ancient Peruvians—an obsession common to the peoples of arid
mountain ranges and deserts in other parts of the world.

The *guanero* (and other sea-birds on the coasts around Lima) is
represented as a god in some way related to the moon, crowned with
an enormous half-moon-shaped diadem. Tello explains that this
moon-bird was supposed to meet the sun on the islands, living with
it and absorbing its fruitful fertilising rays. It would then be sacrificed
to the moon, who thus became goddess of the guano, as the medium
through which she transmitted the fertilising powers of the divinities to the earth.

It is certain that the ancient Peruvians knew the influence of the
moon on the tides, and it was but a short step from here to making her
the great mistress of the ocean, the dispenser of the ocean's wealth.

On the round belly of the pre-Columbian pots we see the moon
as a masked goddess, with a halo of rays shaped like birds' heads,
drops of water, or sirens on a raft or in a crescent-shaped gondola,
holding jars of sea-water. The coastal peoples sprinkled this sea-
water like divine manna on the land at seed-time, sometimes mingled
with fresh water. It is believed that they may have even bartered
sea-water to the people of the sierras for watering their plots on the
steep mountain slopes.

From north to south, the natives of the Peruvian coast, the
cordilleras, and the very heart of the virgin Amazonian forests, seem

to have shared the fear that the Goddess of the Night would devour the sun. The very fact that she was powerful enough to hide it must mean that she was no less important, and when the sun became crimson as it lay on the horizon at dusk, they feared that it was dying and would fall on top of them.

Worst of all, when the sun was victim of an eclipse an over-whelming fear made them cry out and the dogs howl, while drums were beaten to put the aggressor to flight and to save the sun—and themselves—from such a sad end.

Where did the moon go, when she absented herself from the sky several nights running? Well, we are told that she went to another world to chase thieves away.

We should here explain that for the Yungas of the coast, as for the Incas of the Andes, robbery was the most unpardonable vice—so much so that the myth became a fable with a moral. We find the thief depicted as the central star of Orion's belt, being conducted by two gaolers. Four other nearby stars are voracious vultures, about to devour the miserable thief.

We may deduce from this lunar justice that the ancient Peruvians endeavoured to inscribe on the blackboard of the sky the terrible end which awaited the thief on earth. The police were, in fact, surprisingly efficient, and human justice was as implacable as divine justice! No effort was spared until the thief was identified and arrested. We must not forget that the native huts had no locks, and consisted (according to descriptions and illustrations found on pottery) of three walls of bamboo and mud, the fourth side being left open or protected simply by a screen.

Convicted thieves were hanged, but from a sufficiently loose cord to ensure that they should suffer for a long time before dying.

When a burglary was discovered, the alert would be given by attaching heads of corn and green branches to stakes on the road. Guards would be mounted, and soothsayers consulted on the identity of the thief. They, of course, demanded a sacrifice to the moon—preferably a child under five.

A lunar priestess would prepare the altar on the summit of the *waka*. The piping flutes and *sicus* enlivened the ritual dances. One *wako* shows us a child lying on a bed of coloured cotton, decorated with heads of corn and fruit—piled up between the jars of *chicha*. A circle of soothsayers and magicians surround it, while its throat is cut.

This scene recurs a thousand times on the pre-Columbian *wakos*, and such was the obsession with justice that convicted thieves are shown atrociously mutilated.

The moon had at her service numerous priestesses, whom we find depicted on the ritual pottery weaving cotton, spinning rich garments for the priests of the lunar cult, or cleaning and decorating the moon sanctuaries. These priestesses were frequently extremely pretty girls, who were of course fair game for the numerous male soothsayers and magicians. But there was some danger for both partners in such affairs, for we hear of illicit lovers being cast over cliffs on sacred mountains, in the ceremonial presence of priests and other dignitaries. Perhaps jealousy was often the root cause of such punishment!

The moon herself was not without her love affairs, and of course her numerous lovers had to ascend to the sky in order to clasp her. One of the most enterprising was undoubtedly the fox, the most cunning animal of all, who was not content with kissing her but wished to bear her away—and the *wakos* show him tightly clasped by the crescent moon, held in eternal captivity.

Associated in some way with this lunar cult we find toads or frogs depicted on innumerable *wakos*, looking towards the sky occasionally surrounded by clusters of spawn. They symbolise the Yungas' dire need to attract dew and rain to water their fields.

The snake, which so often occurs in the ornamental or symbolic design of the ancient Peruvian culture, is undoubtedly associated with the cult of water because of its zigzag motion, which for the Indian represented lightning, the sign of rain. The Wallas used the snake for magic and curative purposes, and the most beautiful piece of Walla-Marka pottery is probably the very rounded jug in superb red earthenware, highly glazed and decorated by two snakes ready to attack.

Legend tells us that the four gods which appear in the pantheon of the coastal Indians—sun, moon, and their twin children (boy and girl)—were born of a demon dragon living in a large sea-shell. According to tradition the moon laid a cosmic egg which was fertilised by the sun, and the boy born of this union became the father of mankind, while the weak and inferior daughter gave birth to the plants.

The original sea-dragon is illustrated on the *wakos*, and we are told that on leaving the immense sea-shell which was its damp incubator, it walked through the deserts fertilising the arid ground as it went, causing green growth to spring up in its train. From time to time it would cause hurricanes and earthquakes, and have to be placated by human sacrifice.

The ancient peoples of Peru all held the sea-shell in special veneration, endowing it with magic properties. The powder of crushed shells was the offering most appreciated by the pre-Columbian gods. During our travels through the sierras we can still see the Indian village headman blowing into an enormous conical sea-shell, pierced at the apex, as a summons to mass or heralding processions and feast days. The raucous noise thus produced is indeed ideally suited to the wild environment.

It is interesting to note that these mother-of-pearl shells (*strombus galeatus* or pink *spondilus*) are not to be found on the Peruvian coast, but they may well only have been merchandise imported from the Galapagos Islands or from Central America. The Spanish pilot Bartolome Ruiz found on the coast of Equador a large raft put together by the Peruvian Indians, laden with a number of these shells, which the natives believed to be the homes of gods or mythical beings who would provide them with water.

The original hillocks on which the terraced *wakas* were built contain not only the domestic debris, but also many sea-shells. One

of the mummies of Walla-Marka wore round its neck, as a kind of
pendant, a single shell threaded on cotton. For the Indians of these
times, a good blast on one of these shells was reckoned the most
effective way of calling rain or mist. It was this same barbarous sound
which called the people to the *waka* feasts.

The *licenciado* Felipe de Medina tells of his discovery in 1650 of an
idol hidden in a shell near the port of Corquin on the road from
Lima to Callao. He found the 'treasure' while he was in charge of a
group undertaking the demolition of *wakas*, after having removed
an enormous quantity of shells which had been offered to the *waka*.
This 'treasure' consisted of a tiny green idol wedged between two
shells, and accompanied by three tiny green beans.

The fishermen denied any knowledge of the significance of this
idol 'because it was so very ancient' but one of them did at last
admit that it represented one of their ancestors.

Medina expresses his wonder that such a tiny thing, requiring so
much care throughout the centuries, should embody a cult for the
fisherman who worshipped in the *waka* before leaving for the sea.
Intrigued by the presence of the beans in the shell, he learned from the
fishermen that these were the original beans of their species! Undoubtedly they owed their creation to the spirits of the sea, whose
colour was reflected in that of the idol.

Some miles outside Lima near the Herradura—one of the large
beaches of the capital nestling in the curve of a crescent-shaped bay—
we heard of a *waka* which the natives call Choke Ispana. This *waka*
overlooks the sea, and its idol is a monster carved in the rock,
almost square in shape with a snout-shaped muzzle, two little eyes,
and twisted horns. No one knew the origin of this beast, but it may
well have been some kind of amphibious totem.

The *chingungo*, or feline otter, is depicted in countless carvings or
paintings of coastal scenery, enjoying love affairs with young female
wolves and sea lions.

*   *   *

It will be seen how widespread was the great cult of the sea amongst the ancient Peruvians on the Pacific coast. It sprang from the abounding fish, seaweed, and *guaneros* amongst an environment which had—and has—a strange magic: an immense flat expanse of land and sea, silent except for the cries of the sea-birds and the flurry of white foam, set in high relief by the desert beyond. This is the impressive back-cloth to the lives of the ancient inhabitants of the sierras when they visited the coast. As they caught sight of the immense open space from a bend in their downward path, they stopped immediately to implore Mama Cocha (Mother Sea) to keep them free from sickness, so that immediately their business on the plain was concluded they might return to their mountains.

*　　*　　*

The pagan year began between the 24th and 26th of June, when winter suddenly and dramatically takes hold of the land. One evening one may bathe in the pleasantly warm sea, and the next the whole coast may become enveloped in a cold drizzly mist, accompanied by a drastic drop in temperature.

This brutal change from a tropical summer to a miserable damp cold winter—this 'return of ill-fortune'—was anxiously watched for by the Yunga priests from the tops of the *wakas*. After examining the shadow thrown by the pyramid, the priests would announce the celebration of *Onkoy Mita* (feast of the Pleiades) which was accompanied by penitence and prayers.

The *Mosoc Nina*, renewal of the sacred fire of the sun, also marked the pagan new year. This brings us to the star worship of the ancient Peruvians, which came about as a consequence of the nature cult, and which culminated for the Yungas of Chinchaysuyo (the most densely populated Inca region, in which Lima itself is situated) in the extraordinary adoration of the Pleiades, which we find to have exercised a considerable influence on agriculture.

The Pleiades or *Choke Chinchay* symbolised a golden cat which governed all the cats on earth. This constellation, appearing towards the north, was the object of a very influential cult, dating back to remote times. The *Akatay Mita*, the sensual rite to welcome the return of the guano birds and the ripening of the *paltas* of the valley of Rimac, was also celebrated in honour of the Pleiades which protected the sowing of crops, and were therefore called *Chuchokok*.

Young Indian girls, carefully selected for their good looks, danced and played the tambourine, their bodies decorated with discs strategically placed, their heads crowned with feathers and silver sequins, and their throats encircled in tight feather collars. They carried great jugs full of sea-water, which they poured on the thirsty land.

Moon, Sun, and Pleiades being at the head of the divinities worshipped by the peoples of the coast, a succession of stars fell naturally into place, each one symbolising in the sky some important aspect of life on earth. There was no animal or vegetable that the pre-Columbian Indians did not see featured in this celestial book. The llama was naturally included—the only domestic animal of old Peru, and a favourite sacrificial beast.

★   ★   ★

Stars, sea, earth, divine beasts and plants play a constant part in the economic life of these ancient people of the coast around Lima, and have for many thousands of years taken their place among the mythical heroes and idols to which thousands of mummies have borne witness in the symbolic trinkets found among the possessions which accompanied them in the after-life. If Herodotus had known the ancient Peruvians, he would not have told the Egyptians that they were the most religious of all peoples. But how hard it has been to penetrate the mysteries of Peruvian religion! Until quite recently, the history of Peru was virtually considered to be merely the history of the Incas.

Our exploration of the sand-covered pyramids on the Pacific coast undoubtedly only ruffled the surface of these aged sands, from which we have attempted to reconstruct the life of the inhabitants of Peru before the time of the Incas. But it has permitted us to put together in this book a cultural account of a people hitherto forgotten, and only recently rescued from oblivion.

We have seen these ancient mummies brought back to life for a brief spell, before being covered once more by the silent sand where they have lived miraculously protected for so long. It is probable that Peru will preserve her inhabitants better than any other part of the world.

SUPPLEMENT

It was a long and detailed study which led us to climb the long path taken by our Wallas from Lima to Cuzco. This route is about 750 miles long. Some scholars believe that these migratory Wallas came from still further away—from the high plateaux of the Aymaras. This is, however, only a theory, and it seems more probable that they travelled through these parts after having abandoned the Amazonian forest. We may visualise them scaling the mountains like great Arawak conquerors—and indeed some scholars believe they they belonged to the Arawaks.

In his study on the origin of Cuzco, Dr. Luis Valcarcel gives an account of the Viceroy Toledo interrogating fifteen Indians from the city in 1572, who all declared themselves to be Wallas descended from the Wallas of the village of Pachatusan to the south-east of Cuzco, north from San Blas. They all maintained that they had inhabited the spot before the arrival of any Inca, that it was the hostility of the Incas which had forced them to flee with their chief Apo Kalla in search of new land and that they had at length settled where they are to be found to this day, some fifty miles from Cuzco.

Toledo's document fortunately lists the names of some of these Indians. One was called Wampu, which means bargeman; another was Wyma (servant), a third, Utka (retainer), and a fourth, who was then the *Kuraka* of Pisak, was called Pajra (the bald one).

The name of the great chief of the Wallas has proved rather a puzzle, for the spelling alters continually in Toledo's document. We

read Kalla in one place, Kawa or Caua in others, yet again we find
Puccla or even Puglia. We were thus faced with the problem of not
knowing what language these names came from. If we decided on
Aymara, one linguist would translate it as 'the last of the village',
while another would translate it as 'cannon'. In Quechua it might be
'sentry', 'guard', 'spy', but also 'dung'. Aymara and Quechua have
more than twelve thousand words in common.

If we decide on Uru-puquina, we find that Kawa is a canal. We
could then visualise the Wallas in canoes on the Amazonian rivers,
then, after the exodus on the Altiplano of Lake Titicaca, using their
skill to ferry Indians of superior culture on board the delicate *balsas
de totora*. This might also explain the lack of consideration extended
to the Wallas at the time of the first Incas. Speaking of this time,
Martin de Morua, chronicler of the Spanish conquest, reports that
'Cuzco was populated with Lares Indians, Poques, and Wallas, who
were poor people of the lower orders'. Much more recently Pro-
fessor Paul Rivet described the Wallas as 'a frustrated race, living
in servitude'.

These few examples should suffice to illustrate how difficult it is
to write factual history. We finally decided on the name Apo Kalla,
however, as a result of an incident in the tropical valley of Paucartambo, not far from Cuzco. Screaming flocks of tiny green parrots
with red heads crossed our path, and the natives told us that these
kallas were so numerous that they would descend in hordes on cultivated territory and lay whole regions waste, like a plague of locusts.
It is, therefore, quite possible that the Wallas came from here, or at
least stayed here for a long period, for in our *waka* excavations we
found parrot-shaped pottery, and several of the mummies' *ponchos*
were heavily decorated with parrot feathers.

In support of the theory that the Wallas came from the Amazonian
forests we have the reports of the *conquistadores* Polo de Ondegarde
and Father Cobo, who note that 'the Indians from the village of
Walla came from the fourth *waka* called Antuiturco, a great cave
situated at the bottom of the canyon of Patallajta on the road coming

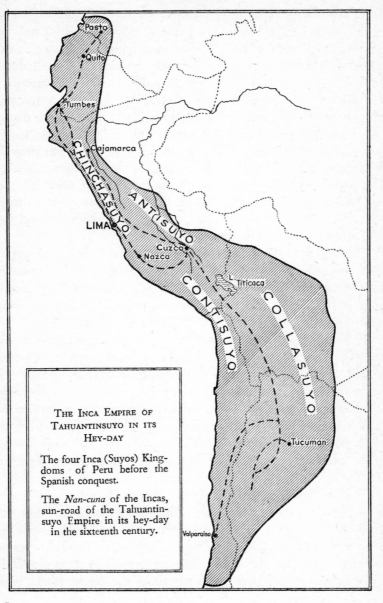

THE INCA EMPIRE OF
TAHUANTINSUYO IN ITS
HEY-DAY

The four Inca (Suyos) Kingdoms of Peru before the
Spanish conquest.

The *Nan-cuna* of the Incas,
sun-road of the Tahuantinsuyo Empire in its hey-day
in the sixteenth century.

from Antisuyo.' Now this Antisuyo is one of four great regions which divide the Inca empire of Tahuantinsuyo, the region in whose virgin forest lived the 'savage' who was supposed to have given the Incas their arrows, their multicoloured feathers, their habit of tattooing, and the cult of the reptiles and jaguars of the forest.

Another voice is raised—that of Garcilaso de la Vega, the love-child of a Spanish captain and an Inca princess, who tells us that the Wallas lived for years in many different places in the forest, lacking any real social structure, living in grottos or in the shelter provided by tangled undergrowth and branches, just like wild beasts, without law or religion, not cultivating the earth, eating acorns and grass, wild fruit, roots, and even human flesh. Garcilaso goes on to say that they habitually went naked, though sometimes covered their bodies with leaves, bark, or animal skins.

This description of course fits many of the Indian tribes of the Amazonian basin. Quechuan etymology gives us a clue, however, for the word Walla is compiled of *Wa* meaning 'tree' and *lla* meaning 'agglomeration'—this reading would be a most fitting description of a race living in tribes in forest regions.

This meaning of *Walla* seems to be almost universally accepted—a swampy tree-covered plain bordering on a river, or a narrow sheltered valley. The idea of freshness, humidity, and green is inherent in the word, which is an interesting point when one considers the tragic aridity of the high Andes. *Walla* can also mean the long pliable straw with which the Indians covered their huts, or decorated their clothes to dance the Wallalli on feast days. It is also a herbaceous plant which grows in the quagmires, the *walla-cajetilla* (*Epibolium denticulatum, var. macro petalum*).

Tello maintained that the Wallas were the first nation to have come from the tropical region—the heights of Paucartambu or from further off still. Once established in Cuzco under Tobay Kapak they may well have forgotten their eastern origin. To Tello perhaps more than anyone else is due the strange urge to trace the Wallas even further afield, beyond Cuzco along the jaguar tracks which may one day have borne this primitive tribe as they emigrated from the vast jungles so many years ago.

So numerous are the traces of the Wallas, from the *selvas* of the Cuzco area through the Cordilleras to Equador, that we were able to discover more than fifty names of towns, villages, lakes, and rivers on the map which actually began or ended in *walla*. We felt that our best plan was to stick to the most important places and facts which could be directly connected with the movement or the origin of the Wallas. We were rewarded with an itinerary rich in surprises and adventures.

★   ★   ★

We hesitated to penetrate the heart of the Amazonian forest— 180 million acres of almost virgin land, crossed by over a thousand rivers! Although there were countless uncharted Indian tracks in this wilderness, we were pretty certain that there was little likelihood of finding any trace of the Wallas there. We decided, however, to take a look at the high Aymaran plateau by Lake Titicaca, some 200 miles as the crow flies from Cuzco.

On one occasion we discovered the name Wallanaku in a book of legends of the Puno district. Who was this mythical hero? The legend of the origin of the town of Saantia was to furnish the answer:

Viracocha and his wife Collawa had four children, two daughters and two sons, destined to people the four corners of the earth. But one of the daughters called Saantia was carried off by a Chaya from the virgin forests of the east. At first she would not accept the advances of this Indian and he decided to kill her, but his brother Wallanaku arrived unexpectedly and saved her.

A tremendous contest between the two brothers took place on a mountain top. They hurtled together to the bottom of an abyss, where they were transformed into raging torrents. Each year, the Indians maintain, beautiful Saantia's ancient lovers renew their epic fight, in the season when the rising currents of Chayanaku and Wallanaku are swollen into swirling torrents by the incessant rain and melting snow from the Cordilleras.

Saantia had two sons by her lovers. Phuyutarqui (winged flute) the son of Chayanaku fathered the Indians of the Amazon forests. Inca Anko, the son of Wallanaku, fathered the people of western Peru, who spread *right to the coast*. These brave and enterprising people were later entrusted by the Incas with the care of the imperial llamas, and in this connection the mysterious word *carhuanco* crops up.

Now it is known that a Walla named Anko played an important role under the Incas, and this mysterious word *carhuanco* came to be associated with the great god Wallallo. It is at least striking that the name of the river and the mountains where the legend was enacted—Callawaya—bears a distinct resemblance to the Carahualla or Carabayllo Indians who live just outside Lima today.

★   ★   ★

In his great history of Peru, Huaman Poma tells us how the Inca Mayta Kapak, Manko's great grandson, undertook the conquest of the 'land of gold', and he mentions specifically the mountains of Callawaya, where the gold was particularly pure.

It is in this land of gold that we find the Wallas on our historic itinerary, much further north, on a cordillera in the Carabaya group—a most dramatic part of country. The mountains are cut by a road, flanked by rugged peaks over thirteen thousand feet high, crowned by the threatening glaciers of Ausangati, and almost perpetually shrouded in mist and clouds. The Indians of these parts deify these mountains and never mention them without making a magic sign.

Here and there, breaking the monotony of the stony and desolate track, muddy puddles reflect the lugubrious if grandiose scenery, very little relieved by the splendour of the snows and the flight of an occasional black and white wader.

What were those people, whose traces range from the high cordilleras to tropical forests, doing in these desolate uplands?

On our first journey from Cuzco to the forest of Quincenil we were stoned by a party of Indians who were returning drunkenly from some festival because we wanted to photograph them, as they pranced along the furrowed track, brandishing long plumes and keeping time to the shrill notes of the reed flutes and the low droning drums. Could *these* be the descendants of our prehistoric Wallas?

We were midway between the lonely villages of Ocongate and Markapata at the time, some 120 miles from Cuzco, at an altitude almost equal to that of Mont Blanc. It is in the vicinity of this singularly unattractive and seldom visited spot that there exist the cyclopean vestiges of a lost city, called Walla-Walla, which is said to mean a succession of pastures. Of these latter (always meagre on the Andes) there remain only very small areas of *ichu*, a sparse dry grass, and the only grass which grows at such altitudes, used as fodder, or for thatching roofs or making palliasses. The waders we saw there were called *wallatas* and the swifts *wallanay*.

The civil and religious remains of the lost city of Walla-Walla show that the inhabitants were of some importance. They overlooked an *abra*, a mountain pass, which an Indian intent on crossing these plateaux could not avoid, and where he would not forget to build a cairn as a tribute to the all-powerful Aukis, the ancestral spirits of the Cordillera, whom it was found wise to placate.

In 1937 attention was suddenly drawn to this desolate spot. A group of roadmenders were at work there, when some of them suddenly stumbled on the 'treasure' of the Wallas, which was subsequently recovered by the Cuzco Archaeological Institute.

The treasure caused such rivalry amongst the roadmenders that Juan Torres, the finder, was obliged to travel as far as the imperial town of the Incas, as Cuzco was called. He went straight to the director of the Archaeological Institute to tell him that one evening while they were on watch, one of his companions had told them about an 'Inca' wall to be found not far from where they were posted at Walla-Walla. Some of the oldest inhabitants of Ocongate were heard to mutter something about 'buried treasure' and 'lost city' in hushed tones. Inevitably the eternal magnetism of gold had strongly attracted the Indian group, so one night, without disturbing their half-bred chief, the roadmenders had gone to the ruins where the monolithic remains still stood, largely buried by soil up to thirteen feet.

The treasure seekers began to dig feverishly, and suddenly something flashed in the beam shed by the lantern: it was a golden idol!

How many centuries had this Walla idol—weighing almost one pound in pure gold—lain there wrapped in a blanket?

'Was there nothing else?' the archaeologist asked Juan Torres. The man hesitated, then admitted that they had been sorely tempted to dig further, but had been overcome with fear—the supernatural fear of ancestral idols disturbed in eternal sleep!

The Indian who had led them to the lost city of the Wallas told them that the gold statuette represented Mama Riti, the Sea Goddess of the perpetual snows of Ausangati, the sacred mountain. Terrified of having unwittingly committed a sacrilege which might well cause them to be cursed by the devils of the Cordillera, the men fled. They arrived back at their work site in the frozen dawn, cowering at the foot of an immense glacier which rose, stark and menacing, above the road.

For several days they did not dare to speak of their adventure even among themselves, while they scrutinised the mountain for any mysterious sign of divine wrath. Then, as no Auki was seen, they wondered what they should do with the golden idol—only to find that it had suddenly and mysteriously vanished.

It took considerable investigation to find out that the idol had been sold in Cuzco for about £1,250 ($3,500), and this is where we came on the scene. We managed to recover the idol, and further excavations brought to light many other relics—several statuettes, jewels, vases and dishes made of silver and gold.

All these precious objects were lovingly wrapped in little *ponchos* made of soft vicuna or alpaca wool, decorated with silver charms. They had been laid in the crevice of a great rock, surrounding the gold idol which the road workers had unearthed.

What race had moulded these features? There was nothing here comparable to the Indians who lived in these wild parts now: a long, angular face with a very pointed chin, almond-shaped eyes, an aquiline nose, and thin lips. If the divinity of Ausangati had plump hands and short fingers, she also had very large calves and feet.

The idol was made in six sections, and was clearly the work of a true artist.

This region was the very heart of the gold country—it is said that most of the Inca gold was taken from here. The Indians were driven out by the Spanish, and sent to work in the mines of Potosi, from where they rarely returned.

We should add that neither gold nor silver had any monetary value in Peruvian times. They were used solely for ceremonial purposes.

What cataclysm shook the valley of Markapata so that the treasure became buried so deeply? About 1700 an earthquake smothered whole villages, and countless men and beasts were lost beneath a flood of mud and stones at the foot of the valley.

The valley remained deserted until 1836, when a mining expedition undertook the search for the mythical hillock (Cerro Kamanti), which according to tradition holds the finest gold, and which naturally they never discovered. But in 1911 the French engineer Letellier confirmed the fantastic wealth of gold in the valley.

★   ★   ★

This valley is not far from the river and virgin forests of Paucartambo, which is held by many historians to be the place from where the Wallas originate. Never a month passes but some adventurer tries desperately to find the famous Paititi, which the chroniclers of the conquest mention so frequently. Legend or reality? Juan Alvarez de Maldonaldo writes that 'the capital of the great Empire of Manu was of gold, of marble, and alabaster'.

Over the years many explorers have come and gone, but recently a party of archaeologists from the University of Arequipa penetrated the forests of the Cuzco region in order to establish, if possible, not only the existence of this fabulous city of Paititi but the truth of allegations made by numerous chroniclers who all spoke of the important archaeological remains of the fortresses to be found on the jungle paths.

While searching for a painting of an Inca on a rock which should point the way to the Imperial Road of a necropolis of four thousand tombs, the expedition stumbled upon a pre-Incan road built and flagged in slate. This they followed for nearly forty miles, and arrived at length at the *tambo* (relay station) called Sucho-Cocha, where the road divides and plunges into the impenetrable forest.

From this road the expedition could see the pre-Inca town of Hualla near Cuzco, not far from the recently discovered Urubamba jungle track, which appeared to have been signposted by the innumerable engravings on the rocks. Though many of these carvings are indistinct, it is perfectly possible to distinguish a great many drawings representing llamas, monkeys, stags, deer, snakes, cocoa leaves, crosses, circles, and an intriguing winged scorpion. It would be interesting to know more about the symbolism of these drawings.

This archaeological site is named Wallanay—a name which comes from rather a typical old legend: the myth of the foundation of Incario—the other name for the Inca Empire. It was written down by a little known Neapolitan Jesuit named Anello Oliva, author of *A History of Peru,* printed in 1631:

> A short time after the Flood the Europeans arrived in America, at Caracas. One party reached Equador, encamping at Santa Elena, as the guests of a chieftain or cacique named Tumbe. Now Tumbe had two children called Quitumbe and Otoya, who quarrelled. Quitumbe went off towards the south with his followers, abandoning his beautiful wife Llira, who was pregnant, but promising to return later. In memory of the errant prince Llira called her son Wallanay, which means 'swallow', and it is from Wallanay that the Incas of Peru are descended.

This, however, is not the end of the story. Old Tumbe set out towards the south, and after founding the town of Tumbes (close to the border of Peru and Equador) he established himself finally on the outskirts of Rimac. The beautiful Llira was about to sacrifice her son Wallanay to the great godhead Pachacamac when an eagle tore off his arms and dropped him on an island where he spent many long years. At last, however, he made himself a raft to reach the mainland, where the natives captured him. The Princess Ciguar saved him and together they fled to a land of flowers, where a son was born to them. The son was called Tome, and he in turn had a son called Atau, whose son Manko became the first Inca of Peru.

In this legend, recounted by the Neapolitan Jesuit, the boy's name is spelt 'Guayanay', in accordance with the custom of the Spanish chroniclers at the time of the conquest. Even today in Peru the name Walla is most often spelt Gualla or Hualla, but we have preferred to use the phonetic form.

★   ★   ★

The sacred valley of Urubamba is where we take up the trail of the Wallas once more, not far from the lost city of Machu Picchu. This has been rediscovered by Hiram Bingham, who later tried to find the tracks which linked it with the higher lost city of the Incas —or even of previous races—whose exact name has been forgotten. A Quechua guide, Ricardo Charaja, discovered traces of a very old road from the top of which the explorers could make out a mega-lithic construction, which crowned a mountain peak of some ten thousand feet.

Following where the road led them, Bingham and his assistant reached the top of the valley, where the old road became broad and paved. Thus they came into the Valley of Wallabamba, which many historians hold as being the Wallas' place of origin or of refuge. One of their chiefs was called Apo Quiraco—which in Quechua means 'cradle'.

*   *   *

On the high plateau called Junin, a little to the north of Lima although still in the Cordillera, the path used by the Wallas to regain the valley of Lima and the coast follows a stream, which in time becomes one of the greatest tributaries of the Amazon. This is the Wallaga.

Perhaps at this point the Wallas once more took recourse to the water. Using rafts or other craft, they may have travelled the length of this long waterway, which splashes from the peaks into the virgin forests and far beyond. Indeed we found many Walla names among the Aguaranas-Jivaros Indians of the river Marañon, into which the Wallaga tumbles. It has even been suggested that the Wallas may have followed the Wallaga and the Amazon to the sea, and peopled the Brazilian island of Marajo.

*   *   *

Still further north from Lima, in the cordilleras which run parallel with the Pacific, there stretches the wonderful Callejon de Huaylas, a long and enchanting green valley which follows the river Santo for 125 miles between the snow-capped peaks of the Cordillera Blanca and the dark summits of the Cordillera Negra. This valley is dotted with enormous eucalyptus trees, and peopled by brightly painted Indians. From this miniature Peruvian Switzerland we descend into the lush Canyon del Pato, from where the Santa leads us to Wallanka.

Thirteen thousand feet higher up, in the little Andean township of Wacclan, lived the beautiful Ninfa, daughter of the *kuraka* of a Walla tribe. Her touching love story is to be found in a collection of legends called *The Stone which Heals the Sickness of Broken Hearts*.

Ninfa lived high up in the mountain village. She had fallen in love with an incredibly ugly young fellow, of whom she was extremely fond. Her father the *Kuraka* was, however, appalled at the prospect of such a *mésalliance*, and poisoned her lover.

Broken-hearted, Ninfa fled towards the coast, but before she had gone far she was struck down with *sonkonane*—an illness common in those whose hearts are broken—and was forced to stop at Kutacocha. An Inca on his way to Quito promised to send her a stone from that town. She was instructed to boil a tiny fragment of this stone in a basin of water whenever the pain recurred, and was assured that the stone had wonderful healing powers.

The Inca kept his word. Ninfa kept the stone in a corner of her house, and used it to her great benefit. She also offered this cure to anyone suffering from the same complaint! Thus the stone has gradually shrunk in size, for every Indian of Callejon de Huaylas who was suffering from a broken heart tried the remedy.

Having seen the name 'Walla' blazoned over the sierras and the jungles, we finished our tour and returned to Cuzco.

How long had the Wallas lived peacefully in the heart of the Cuzco valley before being disturbed by the approach of the Incas? The chronicler Sarmiento de Gambao tells us that they had had time to organise themselves into little tribal or family groups, and had been cultivating their fields for several centuries. We hear now they were found on the slopes of the valley of Cuzco 'where the sun rises', and 'which was peopled solely by Walla Indians'. We are furthermore told that they were of friendly and peaceful disposition.

Thus it was that Apo Kalla—or Puccla—and his people camped peacefully on the edge of the vast swamp at Wallay Pata (here history and linguistics agree perfectly) in a pink glade of the gentle Cuzco valley, encircled by rounded hills, russet-coloured and denuded of vegetation, rising to heights of some eleven thousand feet. These mountains assured Cuzco—the centre of the Inca world— of a temperate climate for most of the year, although on occasions the nights could be very cold and noon could be very hot. Four rivers keep the region well watered; one of these, the Huatanay, the sacred river of Cuzco, is named Puri-Walla-Mayu in its lower reaches, at the exact spot where the Wallas camped. This means 'the river meandering over the plain'.

The superb peak of Sacsahuaman towers above the swamp, protecting it and forming a splendid amphitheatre of mountains—quite impregnable on three sides because of deep gulfs and ravines.

Against this dramatic background we may imagine the Wallas busy plucking the golden maize, which in good years was covered with grain throughout almost the whole length of the stalk. The Inca Manko was delighted by the fertility of this valley after the barren uplands of his native land, and the wide expanse of golden grain must indeed have been an impressive sight.

Here and there Wallas grew coca bushes, with their small waxy green leaves, and full furrows of brilliant red pimentos.

Among the women whom Manko had brought with him to the valley was the cunning, cruel, and ruthless Mama Wako. Like others she was delighted with what she saw. Manko himself, sceptre in hand, was already dreaming of settling down with his wandering people in this pleasant valley. This woman is said to have initiated the Incas into idolatry, of which they had been hitherto ignorant.

'She was thought of as a magician,' writes Huaman Poma, 'and she claimed to be able to make stones, trees, birds, lakes and sticks talk. In this way she lured the Indians to speak with devils, and by means of strange powers she misled not only the people of Cuzco, but many others who fell under her spell.'

By way of completing this damning portrait, Huaman Poma describes her as being 'extremely good-looking, dark-complexioned, fairly tall, always dressed in pink decorated with large silver brooches ... revered and served by all'. Then, as though reluctant to leave any part of her character shrouded in mystery, the author goes on: 'She gave herself to any man who desired her without class distinction', and she was given the title of coya—'the first woman of the Incas and the Queen of Cuzco'.

Manko Kapak founded the Inca empire. Most of the chroniclers say that Mama Oɔclo was Manko's sister and wife. Huaman Poma, however, says that Mama Wako was not only his principal wife but also his mother.

Mama Wako listened to Manko's plans: he would build a temple to the Sun Father at the juncture of the two rivers; round this temple he would build the city from which he would rule over the neighbouring tribes. He hoped that the tribes would become his subjects of their own free will, and enable him to conquer without using force. Manko then explained his plan to drain water from the swamp, and bring a great deal more land under cultivation.

He described the future capital with the eloquence of a visionary. With the point of his gold stick he drew a puma—the most sacred beast—in the soil. The area where the puma's heart would be represented the vast marshy plain, where his people would celebrate the great seasonal and agricultural festivals together with the subject tribes. The outline of the puma's body represented the two rivers, where would arise the different quarters of the city—one part being reserved for the aristocracy, another for the artisans. Sacsahuaman marked the head, and the river Vilkamayo was drawn like the tail.

The sacred city was thus to be built on the site belonging to the primitive Wallas, who were at that moment busy bringing in their crops. It was necessary to eject them. Manko's war-cry, which sounded like the howl of the four clans whom he was leading into battle, was echoed by a blood-curling yell from Mama Wako, whose name has become a symbol of brutality.

Mama Wako threw herself into the fray. The Wallas, who were used to seeing their fertile swamp respected by their neighbours, now tried vainly to defend themselves against the invaders. One of the harvesters sprang forward to defend the field into which the enemy were advancing. Mama Wako swung her sling and hurled a lump of gold (probably only a stone) at the fellow's legs. He stumbled and fell, and before he could rise Mama Wako ripped open his throat with a sharp stone and smeared her face in hot blood before the eyes of his horrified companions.

Just for an instant the Wallas paused in horror, but they were no warriors, and Mama Wako wanted easy victory. She tore open the breast of the dead man and, scooping out the lungs, blew them up and brandished them aloft like some hideous trophy. Finally she tore the heart from the corpse and took it between her teeth; with her features twisted into the most terrifying and bloodthirsty mask, screaming and covered with blood, she put the natives to flight.

Was Manko burdened with a conscience? It is doubtful if this horrible victory troubled him much, for he tackled the situation with surprising diplomacy. Realising that if news of this crime reached the ears of neighbouring tribes he and his followers would be regarded as butchers, he decided that full-scale massacre was the order of the day. Thus he and his people spent the following night in dreadful slaughter—killing even the unborn children of the miserable Wallas, so that no sign of them should remain.

This spectacular *dénouement* of a tale of horror satisfied the chroniclers of the conquest, who concluded that the Wallas disappeared completely and were never heard of again. A more probable assumption, however, would be that this struggle for land (undoubtedly bloodthirsty and probably a much longer affair than one is led to believe) only marked the end of the Wallas' reign and the setting up of Cuzco by Manko. Some historians believe that the Wallas were expelled from Cuzco not by Manko Kapak, but by his son Sinchi Roka.

The fighting, in fact, went on for several centuries and was not limited to the Cuzco area, but extended as far as Lima. Groups formed of hunted people who had been driven from Cuzco, or who were about to be invaded by the constant onward surge of the Incas. Leading these groups we find Ankawallo, head of the desperate Chankas and other tribes who sought to bar the way against the Inca army at Andahuaylas. Leaving the women, children and the aged behind, thousands of Indians gathered together on the banks of Lake Choclo-Cocha. But the Inca leader sent his sister to seduce Ankawallo and kill him, thus winning a great victory with little bloodshed.

Huaman Poma tells us that after Ankawallo's death, part of his people submitted to the conquerors The others fled over the mountains to the north, where they settled.

It is pretty clear that every member of the family had a part to play in the warfare of those days, and sex was by no means despised as a weapon. The invading wave of Incas swept on from Cuzco to Jauja, some 560 miles away, and only 150 miles from Lima.

Here we find the opposing Walla and Inca forces. Not to be outdone in sex warfare, the Walla leader sent his extremely beautiful sister to the Inca leader, Tupca Yupanki. During the night the girl overheard Inca plans for slaughtering the sleeping Wallas, and slipped quietly away in time to warn her people. When the Incas attacked there was not a Walla to be found.

*　　*　　*

It is almost certain that the vast majority of Wallas had by this time been driven out from Cuzco. The Spanish chroniclers are, however, quite inaccurate when they maintain that all trace of them was lost. Huaman Poma repeatedly mentions the 'captains' and 'chiefs' of the Inca army known as Wallawisas. It seems probable that these were Wallas who were respected by the Incas for their splendid fighting qualities, or who had helped them as spies and informers. Huaman Poma mentions Wallawisas again when he describes the laws of the Inca government which was set up in Cuzco. One of these laws was:

> It is ordained that a chief priest or sorcerer shall be appointed in this great city, capital of all our kingdom. This sorcerer shall be called Wallawisa. Other sorcerers shall be appointed throughout the kingdom, whose duty it will be to carry out the will of the gods and idols. These priests and sorcerers will keep themselves informed of everything that is going on in the world.

Then we find the Kolla-Wallas, who acted as witch-doctors for the Incas, and from whom are descended the famous witch-doctors of the high Aymaran plateau by Lake Titicaca—who even bear the same name.

Indeed, the belief of the Spanish chroniclers that all trace of the Wallas had vanished seems sheer nonsense, for not only were they allotted plots of land, but they were honoured by Inca titles.

There are documents in the historic archives of Cuzco pertaining to the distribution of land, carried out in 1595 'among all the Indians of the valley, at Yulay, Wallambamba, and Urubamba'. Most of these Indians bear indisputably Walla names.

We read, for example, that Miguel Puccla (many Indians were baptised with Christian names by the Spanish missionaries at an early date) received two *topos*—areas where maize was planted. Xpoval Pulu-Puccla, Lucas Guanti-Puccla, Goncalo Katao Puccla, and so on appear in the lists. Among these Indians 'chosen to become Incas of this land' figures the name Don Alonso Pucclana—a name we also come across in Lima, and which has been given to the largest of the Walla pyramids. This man was in fact chief of his Majesty's *Yana-conas*, which might be translated as majordomo of the servants employed by the *conquistadores*.

The plots of land and little Andean villages in the sacred valley of the Incas bear even today names which are reminiscent of their origin—names such as Chuqui-Ucra-Walla, Walla-Miaca, Quiska-Walla.

Assuredly the Wallas did not cease to exist, for there is no doubt that their descendants live there today.

PRE-COLUMBIAN CHRONOLOGY OF THE
PERUVIAN PACIFIC COAST

It is impossible to ascertain a chronology for the long pre-Columbian history with as much accuracy as we can chronicle the period following the Spanish conquest. There were no documents. It has not been possible to decipher inscriptions in the way we have been able to do for the Mayas or Egyptians, the Greeks or the Romans.

We can, therefore, give only a very rough approximation to dates, and there can be no universally accepted dates. For instance, Tello placed Chavin culture at c. 1000 B.C., while several American archaeologists place it in the first century A.D. Tiahuanaco culture, which is often dated about A.D. 1000, was reckoned by Postnanslay to be 13,000 years old.

It might be thought that carbon 14 would enable us to ascertain easily the age of a piece of material, a fragment of wood or bone, or remnants of plants, with a margin of error not more than 200 years. But certain doubts have recently been thrown on the accuracy of carbon 14.

In order to play safe, therefore, we are giving here not one single chronology, but various sequences selected from accepted and recent authorities:

W. C. BENNETT (1949)
Chavin:	1200 B.C. to A.D. 400
White-On-Red:	A.D. 400
Maranga:	A.D. 400–1000

M

Tiahuanaco: A.D. 1000–1300
Chancay: 1300–1438
Inca: 1438–1532

GORDON WILLEY (1958)

Chira-Villa (simple pottery):   2000 B.C.
Old Ancon. Supe. Maranga 1:   1000 B.C.
Maranga 2–3:   About the time of Christ
Middle Ancon: Tiahuanaco
   on the coast: A.D. 500
Late Ancon: Late Chancay: A.D. 1000
Inca: c. 1500

HENRI LEHMANN (1953)

Aspero-Chilca (?)   3000 B.C. (beginnings of agriculture)
Old Ancon: White-On-Red: 800 B.C. (formation of cultures)
Old Lima: c. 600 B.C. (zenith)
Late Ancon-Chancay: 1200–1450 (blending of cultures; forma-
                           tion of villages)
Inca-Chancay: 1450–1521 (imperialist and militarist)

P. VILLAR CORDOVA (1955)

Culture	Around Lima	Coastal Strip	Dates
Primitive	Kauqui	Prehistoric fishing culture	Early centuries of the Christian era
Pre-Tiahuanaco	Yauyos and Attawillos combine with Chavin	Pre-Lima	c. A.D. 500–1000
Tiahuanaco and 'Epigonals'	Spread of the Andean Culture of the Colla Indians on the coast	Chancay	c. A.D. 1000–1400
Inca	Submission of the Andean chieftains to the Incas	Submission of the coastal chieftains to the Incas	A.D. 1400–1430
	Inca *tambos* in the high valleys	Inca building Local governments under Inca authority	A.D. 1430–1535 (coming of the Spaniards)

MAX UHLE

4 phases of proto-Lima culture:
I Pre-proto-Lima
II Proto-Lima Maranga-Chancay
III Proto-Lima Nieveria (Cajamarquilla)
IV Tiahuanacan Proto-Lima

NOTE ON THE DEVELOPMENT OF CIVILISATION
ON THE PERUVIAN COASTAL STRIP

We have compared various reports (including the evidence of carbon 14 dating), and have attempted to give a rough chronological table. It must be realised, however, that this is neither definitive nor complete.

Dates	Period	Culture
c. 4500–3000 B.C.	Pre-agricultural and pre-pottery	Fishing is the economic foundation of life. Primitive food-gathering and hunting
		Small semi-subterranean encampments along river-banks. Rudimentary weaving of vegetable fibres, reeds, dried grain, even seaweed and hair
		Immense ceremonial ponchos in variegated feathers
		Plain and chequered basket-work—baskets, mats, quivers
		Bone objects from bones of animals, birds, and fish. Numerous objects from stones of various kinds, including obsidian, quartz, lapis-lazuli, turquoise, jade; shells, coral, fish-teeth
		Fish nets made from loops of cotton, reeds or dried seaweed
		Reed rafts, or boats made from inflated seal-skins
		Red and yellow vegetable dyes

Dates	Period	Culture
c. 3000–2000 B.C.	Horticultural	Fishing still the economic basis
		Cotton. Beans
		Further development of weaving in fibre and hair
		Use of animal skins for clothing—fox, seal, jaguar, etc.
		The art of the feather
		Pyramids built for religious purposes in the centre of villages, at oases, and at the junctures of rivers
		Very fine basket-work. Wooden weapons and tools
		Birth of metallurgy. Use of gold and silver in making masks, little bells, trinkets, ritual objects, breast-plates, gauntlets, crowns, etc.
c. 2000 B.C.–A.D. 200	Birth of agriculture and pottery	Fishing is still of fundamental importance
		Maize, manioc, cotton, beans, groundnuts, pasturage
		Villages of little mud huts
		More pyramids built—religion becomes more organised
		Hill fortifications defend the entrances to valleys
		Communication routes are opened up for the purposes of trade with the Amazon and Andes regions
		Irrigation canals
		Weaving becomes a specialist craft—wool and cotton
		Symbolic art — sculpture — metalworking, particularly in beaten gold —alloys of gold and copper, copper and tin

Dates	Period	Culture
c. A.D. 200–1000	Regional cultures flourish. Development of agriculture	Numerous cultural associations spiral right up into the foothills of the Andes Hydraulic working The pyramids become burial places Fertilisation of the ground by guano and fish-heads Tiny autonomous states existing in each valley, under theocratic control Separate military, political and religious chiefs Developments of castes and specialist trades Smelting of metal, manufacture of mud bricks, copper tools and arms Realist and symbolic art—portraits of living people, stylised representations of demons Head-hunting a by-product of warfare Red, blue and yellow paste colours
c. A.D. 1000 et seq.	Expansion of Tiahuanaco culture	Rapidly growing population grouped in kingdoms and confederations, situated at the heads of the valleys rising from the coast—possibly forming a sort of coastal empire Villages protected by high walls Roads marked out with stakes or little walls Organisation of military forces Sanctuaries and pilgrimages Considerable spread of trade Hey-day of the Wallas, Huanchos, Pachacamacs Numerous influential oracles. Countless priests. Religious organisation crystallised

Dates	Period	Culture
c. A.D. 1000 et seq.—continued		Pottery both utilitarian and ceremonial. Design based on botanical or marine themes
c. A.D. 1300–1400	Chancay and Huaura dominate right up to the Inca conquest	Local despotic kingdoms. Huge fortresses built. Military organisation for wars of expansion Castes and social classes meticulously laid down in the urban agglomerations. Hereditary nobility. Coastal navigation on huge rafts and floats Orchards and plantations Further development of metallurgy—use of bronze and lead Relief decoration and geometric design on walls and pottery
c. 1400 et seq.	Inca conquest	The Incas impose their rule, military and civil organisation, a rigid administration system and impose a monopoly of trade and the arts Systematic storing and division of produce The religion of the sun tolerates the gods of the assimilated peoples Tools and weapons of bronze Ceramic decadence

GLOSSARY OF QUECHUA, AYMARA, AND SPANISH WORDS

Acequia	Trench dug for crop irrigation.
Adobe	Brick made of sun-dried earth.
Alcalde	Indian governor or headman.
Altiplano	Very cold high plateau (about 13,000 feet above sea-level).
Amauta	Inca wise man.
Andenes	Cultivated terraces on the slopes of the Andes.
Antisuyo	The north-east region of the Inca empire.
Apacheta	A pile of flat stones which the Indians built up to persuade the mountain spirits to let them pass by.
Aukis	Guardian spirits of the Andes.
Ayllu	An agrarian community.
Aymara	A pre-Columbian race, and culture. There are still *c.* 50,000 Aymaras living on the shores of Lake Titicaca.
Balsas de Totora	Gondolas made of woven weeds, used by fishermen on Lake Titicaca.
Barbacoa	Protective covering of bamboo placed in front of mummy.
Camote	Sweet potato.
Campa	Semi-civilised tribe from the Peruvian Amazon.
Cancha	Grilled grains of Indian corn.
Cerro	Hill or hillock.
Chamico	Shrub producing poisonous drug.
Chavin	Ancient civilisation to the north of Lima, *c.* 1000 B.C.
Chicha	An intoxicating drink, made from corn, not unlike beer.
Chinchasuyo	North-west region of the Inca empire.
Chinkana	Labyrinth, underground tunnels or galleries.
Chonta	Species of palm tree, with a very hard dark wood.

Chullo	Pointed hat made in multicoloured wool with earflaps.
Chullpa	Stone Age funeral tower.
Coca	A leaf which was worshipped by the Incas but which has become equivalent of chewing-gum to the Indian since the Spanish conquest.
Cochimilco	Doll-shaped clay idol.
Collasuyo	South-west region of the Inca empire.
Contisuyo	Western region of the Inca empire.
Cushma	Loose tunic worn by Amazon Indians.
Cuzco	Capital of the Inca empire.
Cuy	Peruvian guinea-pig.
Encomiendas	System of forced labour on the land or in the gold and silver mines under the Spanish colonisation.
Fardo	Funeral wrappings to enclose a mummified figure.
Guano	Natural fertiliser; the excrement of sea-birds found mainly along the Pacific coast of Peru.
Garua	Winter mist in the Lima area, due to the cold Humboldt current.
Huaca	See *Waka.*
Huarango	A kind of acacia growing along the sandy coast.
Huayno	A Quechua dance of Inca origin.
Huayco	An avalanche of mud mixed with stones and ice.
Hunu	Inca group of 10,000 families.
Hunukamayoc	Inca ruler of a *hunu.*
Ichu	Plant used as fodder in the high valleys of the Andes.
Inca	One of the greatest pre-Spanish civilisations, the Inca empire centred on Cuzco, spread from the south of Columbia across Ecuador, Peru, Bolivia, and a part of Chile and Argentina. This empire was at the height of its glory at the end of the eleventh century. Its emperor held supreme power, and history has recorded the names of fourteen emperors before the Spanish conquest.
Kantuta	*Cantua buxifolia Juss*, the Inca flower, red or yellow.
Kipu	An Inca mnemonic aid consisting of woollen cords of various colours and thicknesses.
Kollas	Inhabitants of Collao on Lake Titicaca—a very ancient race.

Kullpis	Burial towers in the mountains around Lima.
Kuraka	The chief of a Walla tribe, or *ayllu*.
Lima	The capital of Peru, founded by Pizarro on 18th January 1535. It is on the shores of the Pacific and has over 1,700,000 inhabitants.
Lobos Marinos	Peruvian seals
Lucumo	*Lucumo obovata (sapotaceae)*. The Quechua *rukma*—a kind of fruit.
Llama	Cud-chewing mammal, native to the Peruvian mountains, and basis of the Indian economy in these parts.
Llauto	An Inca turban which varies according to the clan.
Lliclla	Multicoloured cloak worn by Indian women in the Andes. The back is folded over, making a pouch in which the wearer can carry a load of food or a baby.
Mallki	Name given to the ancestral mummies in mountain regions.
Manko Kapak	The first of the Inca emperors, founder of the dynasty.
Maremoto	Sudden violent sea-storm due to submarine earthquake.
Mashiguengas	Indian tribe from the high Urubamba (Amazon region).
Mate	*Lagenaria vulgaris*. Empty gourd, sometimes vase-shaped.
Mitimaes	Tribes moved by the Incas to another region than their own either as a punishment or as a method of colonisation.
Mochadero	A chapel or temple, coming from *Mochar*—to adore (Quechua).
Mochica	or *Proto-Chimu*. An ancient civilisation of the northern coast, famous for its magnificent pots with portrait designs on them.
Molle or Mulli	A woodland pepper tree with pink seeds and delicate foliage.
Munao	Name given to ancestral mummies along the coast.
Nan-cuna	Name given to the famous Inca roadway which covered about 30,000 miles of desert and mountain land, and comprised countless bridges across ravines and gulfs as well as tunnels going under the Andes themselves.
Nazca	Ancient culture of the southern coast, famous for its fine multi-coloured *wakos* (pottery). An agricultural people who irrigated their lands by means of deep wells and aqueducts.
Oca	An edible root growing in the Andes.
Onkoy	Illness (Quechua).
Pacae	*Inga feuillei (leguminosae)*. Tree known as guaba on the coast.
Pachacamac	Ancient Peruvian divinity of the central coastal regions. Now the remains of a town, 30 miles to the South of Lima.

Palla	Inca woman of noble blood.
Paracas	Centre of an ancient civilisation, celebrated for its remarkable weaving which is unique throughout the world.
Pariakaka	A god of the Yauyos in the Andes above Lima.
Pariana	Sentinel of crops.
Pisak	Vast remains of a Stone Age fortress in the sacred valley of the Incas (Rio Urubamba or Vilcanota).
Porra	Heavy pointed stone weapon.
Pukara	Pre-conquest fortress or tower.
Puma	Carnivorous member of the cat family—adopted as a totem by the Incas.
Puna	The high peaks of the Andes.
Purucalla	Funeral honours.
Puruchucu	From the word *pur* meaning a helmet. An ancient pre-Inca palace which was reconditioned by the Incas.
Puschka	Spinning staff.
Quebrada	Canyon or deep gorge with a road passing through it.
Quechua	Inhabited temperate region of the Andes.
Quena	Indian flute made of bone or reed.
Quinoa	*Chenopodium quinoa*, or Inca corn, which grows at high altitudes.
Rimac	River and valley in which Lima is situated.
Runanakak	'The one who makes people suffer.' Official in charge of public confession at *waka* festivals.
Sacsahauman	A gigantic fortress which dominated Cuzco and was made up of three stone ramparts made of great blocks of stone each weighing more than twenty tons and held up solely by means of their perfect positioning.
Sandia	Name of river and town in the Puno region, near Lake Titicaca.
Selva	Amazon forests covering three-fifths of Peru—a vast area.
Serrano	An inhabitant of the sierra.
Sierra	Mountain region of the Andes covering thirty-two per cent of Peru.
Sicu	Indian pipes of Pan played by the Indians of the high plateaux.
Tahuantinsuyo	The Inca empire of four regions (*suyos*).
Takkla	Primitive wooden spade.
Tambo	Inca relay station.

Tiahuanaco	Stone Age civilisation of the Bolivian high plateaux. It is famous for its 'sun-gate', but the people who actually built this are unknown.
Tiana	Sort of sedan chair.
Titicaca	The highest navigable lake in the world, over 12,000 feet above sea-level and about 570 miles from Lima. It covers more than 5,000 square miles, is 94 miles long, and contains 36 sizable islands. It is a paradise for trout which have been caught up to four feet in length.
Tocricuc	Inca elected controller of a confederation of tribes, villages, and settlements.
Topo	Ancient agricultural measurement.
Tupu	Long silver pin shaped like a soup spoon.
Totora	Reed growing on Lake Titicaca.
Urus	Primitive Indian tribe living on the shores of Lake Titicaca. Now fast becoming extinct.
Vigogne	*Auchenia vicuna.* A ruminant of the llama genus of the camel family whose wool is the silkiest, finest and most expensive in the world.
Viracocha	The supreme divinity in the Inca religion.
Waka	or *Huaca.* Sacred pyramid or burial place along the Peruvian coast. In the mountains the name was given to anything which might be used as a totem of worship because of some unusual feature.
Wako	Pre-Columbian ceremonial pottery.
Walla	An ancient tribe. A damp prairie-land.
Yanaconas	Servant caste.
Yungas	Tropical lowlands and the people who live there.